FROM

GOD'S GLORY

REDISCOVERING FAITH AND FOCUS AFTER LOSS

*Special **FREE** Bonus Gift for You*

To help you to achieve more success, there are

FREE BONUS RESOURCES for you at:

www.for-gods-glory.com

•3 in-depth videos that will lead you to a life in Christ that honors and glorifies Him

PAT BARRINGTON

Copyright © 2023 **Pat Barrington**

All rights reserved. No part of this book or its associated ancillary materials may be reproduced or transmitted in any form or by any means, electronic or mechanical, including photocopying, recording, or by any informational storage or retrieval system, without prior permission from the author.

Printed in the United States of America

WHAT OTHERS ARE SAYING ABOUT PAT

"Dr. Pat Barrington is among the finest people I have been privileged to work with over the years. She has a great heart for people and is deeply gifted by God to share the Gospel in a winsome and effective manner. Pat speaks with authority from her wide knowledge of the Word of God, and she loves… like Jesus told us to love – with deep compassion and a desire to see everyone find hope in the person of Jesus. If you read this book, you will find hope to continue forward, even in difficult times… going from grief to God's glory." —**Bill Cordrey, Pastor.**

"Pat Barrington is a blessing to me. She has had a big impact on my life. I know her book will lead you to a deeper walk with the Lord and help you overcome the challenges in your life." —**Tim A. Cummins, Director-Whirlwind Missions.**

"Having known Pat since 1980, I can say that her life exemplifies the truths of God's Word. She shares how you can also live in victory."–**Earl Stephenson, Pastor.**

"Having known Pat as a Christian physician and as her pastor, I know that she has a heart for God and for sharing the message of Jesus. Her message is life-changing!" **-Dr. David Poe, Retired Pastor.**

"Pat's life is consistent with what she teaches. She is transparent in her failures as well as her successes. You will learn from her personal stories as well as the truths she shares. Pat's personal journey will provide the reader with insights into developing strategies designed to address loss from a Christian perspective."- **Dr. Bob Mills, Retired Executive Director of the Kansas-Nebraska Convention of Southern Baptists.**

"Pat Barrington is an example of a Spirit-filled Christian! She shares from her experiences to draw you closer to Christ." **-Dr. Greg Cruce, Pastor Rock Bridge Baptist Church**

"Pat Barrington is a Warrior-Servant for Christ. I served alongside Pat in the Amazon Jungle of Peru as she served the precious people through medical care and a gospel witness. The Lord is at work in and through Pat. I'm so grateful for her." - **Jeff Holeman, Minister of Mission Strategy, First Baptist Church Oxford.**

"I have known Dr. Pat Barrington for almost 40 years. Her husband, Carl, and I were best friends up to his death from cancer in 2019. Over the years, I was privileged to observe Carl and Pat as they labored tirelessly through various ministries in Texas and Georgia. Pat has always seen her life and vocation as intentional platforms for the proclamation of the gospel. I can recall Carl smiling as he spoke about the many ways that Pat shared Christ as a medical doctor, women's ministry leader, neighbor, missionary, and friend. I can promise that whatever Pat does, she will do it with her whole heart. Much like her Lord, she is a special person with a unique ability to embrace the plight of hurting people. In doing so, lives are transformed, and people are saved! No doubt, this is her life's calling!"- **Dr. David A. Wheeler, Professor of Evangelism, Sr. Executive Director of LU Shepherd, Rawlings School of Divinity.**

"Pat has the unique ability to speak as a medical professional and also as one who has walked through the deep waters to personal loss and grief to help us see the radiant hope of God's goodness and steadfast comfort and peace."- **Mike Riggins SHRM-CP, PHR.**

"Pat's husband, Carl, was a dear friend. He was an incredibly talented and smart man who was Pat's wonderful complimentary partner, best friend, emotional rock, spiritual leader, and, most of all, husband to Pat. Are you unsure what to do next after such a huge loss in life? Pat has walked this road and will guide you back to a life of joy and thriving!" - **J. Mark Perry, Music Pastor, First Baptist Church, Powder Springs, Georgia.**

MOTIVATE AND INSPIRE OTHERS

SHARE THIS BOOK

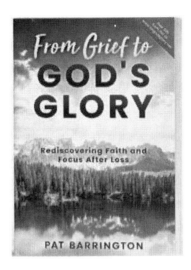

Retail price: $14.99

Special Quantity Discounts:

5-20 copies	$12.99
21-99 copies	$11.99
100-499 copies	$10.99
500-999 copies	$9.99
1000+ copies	$7.99

To order bulk copies:

www.for-gods-glory.com

THE IDEAL PROFESSIONAL SPEAKER FOR YOUR NEXT EVENT!

Any organization that wants to develop its people to become "extraordinary" needs to hire Pat Barrington for a keynote and/or workshop training!

TO CONTACT OR BOOK PAT BARRINGTON TO SPEAK:

www.for-gods-glory.com

THE IDEAL COACH FOR YOU!

If you're ready to overcome challenges, have major breakthroughs, and achieve higher levels, then you will love having Pat Barrington as your coach!

TO CONTACT:

www.for-gods-glory.com

Dedication

It is with respect, admiration, and sincere appreciation that I dedicate this book to my wonderful family. Without you and the lessons you have taught me throughout my life, I would not have the blessing of being where I am today. Thank you from the bottom of my heart! I love you dearly!

Theo and Autumn

Ben, Michelle, Theo and Autumn

Michelle, Me, Autumn, Joyce, Ben, and Theo

Holli, Sherri, Me, Bill, Natalie, Steve, and Teressa

My Extended Hulsey Family

Contents

Dedication x

A Message to You! 1

Chapter 1: Regain Focus on God 6

Chapter 2: Talk to God 16

Chapter 3: Know and Stand on Truth 26

Chapter 4: Worship 37

Chapter 5: Do for Others 48

Chapter 6: Let Your Friends Help 55

Chapter 7: Family Matters 62

Chapter 8: Plan for Your Future and Trust God for It 69

Chapter 9: It's Okay to Cry and Grieve 76

Chapter 10: Do What You Need to Do 81

Chapter 11: Don't Isolate 86

Chapter 12: Have Fun 92

Chapter 13: Get Right With God 98

Contents

Chapter 14: Find Your Purpose 103

Chapter 15: Listen to God's Voice..112

Chapter 16: Be Filled With the Holy Spirit.......................119

Chapter 17: Give Glory to God 127

Chapter 18: Discipline Your Mind......................................134

One Last Message! 143

Acknowledgments 146

About Pat 149

A Message to You!

When I was just 18 years old, attending the University of Oklahoma on my way to the Baptist Student Union, a good friend named Susan introduced me to Carl Barrington. Both of us were wide-eyed freshmen, and our connection was instant. We embarked on our journey together, as students and as a couple, just a week after our first meeting. Our lives were woven together in a beautiful tapestry of shared experiences throughout our college years.

We found ourselves side by side in the university marching band, raising our voices in the college choir at First Baptist Church in Norman, Oklahoma, and embarking on several choir trips. However, it was more than that. It was the countless meaningful conversations, the shared dreams, and the challenges we tackled together. It didn't take long for me to realize that Carl was "the one."

What began as dating swiftly blossomed into a deep and enduring love affair. As we graduated college, our love story evolved into a beautiful marriage. We were more than husband and wife; we were best friends and partners in every sense of the word. Together, we pursued our higher education and ventured into our respective careers. Carl answered the call to become a minister while I pursued my calling as a family practice physician and missionary.

I can't begin to express just how deeply I adored him. I envisioned growing old together, and we set out to make the most of every moment. Our shared passion for exploring the world led to countless adventures, each one adding a new chapter to our story. Life was a grand tapestry of excitement and joy, especially as we welcomed our only child, Michelle, into the world. Becoming grandparents to Theo and Autumn was an added delight that warmed our hearts.

However, life took an unexpected turn when Carl was diagnosed with an aggressive form of prostate cancer at the age of 50. Our world was suddenly dominated by doctors' appointments, medical consultations, and treatments. We spared no effort, seeking specialists from all corners of the globe and exploring cutting-edge therapies. In support of

Carl, I made the difficult decision to retire from my medical practice at age 62, becoming his dedicated caregiver.

Despite our best efforts, the cancer metastasized, and we found ourselves on a challenging path. Carl enrolled in a clinical trial, and while the treatment offered hope, its side effects left him anemic, necessitating weekly blood transfusions. It became a battle against the relentless progression of the disease.

With heavy hearts, we made the choice to transition to hospice care, where Carl could find comfort and peace in the familiarity of home. Just three short days later, at the age of 63, he embarked on his next great adventure to heaven, leaving behind a void that seemed hard to fill.

Before this chapter of profound loss, our lives had been marked by boundless energy, excitement, and the shared pursuit of our dreams. We were a dynamic couple, partners in faith, life, and love, embracing every opportunity to make a difference with many mission trips and ministries as we savored the beauty of God's world.

However, when Carl departed for his heavenly home, my world turned upside down. I found myself thrust into the relentless throes of grief—grief not only for his passing but also for the loss of a future that had been painstakingly planned together. The dreams of our remaining years and of celebrating our 50th wedding anniversary together were forever shattered. The weight of his absence and the stark realization of my new status as a widow left me feeling ill-equipped to deal with loneliness and isolation.

I can vividly recall the moment I first had to check a box on a form that read "widow." The weight of that single word pressed heavily on my heart as if it encapsulated the enormity of my situation. Becoming a widow wasn't just a change in marital status; it was a profound life-altering experience. The waves of grief threatened to pull me under. I yearned for help but scarcely knew how to ask for it.

Navigating the turbulent waters of loss is a formidable challenge. I wished someone had given me guidance or a roadmap to navigate this uncharted territory. The enormity of the situation was overwhelming, but I knew I needed to find my way through it.

Through this journey of grief, I discovered a series of vital steps that gradually led me from darkness to hope and ultimately to giving glory to God. These steps became my lifeline, helping me regain my focus on God, reignite my conversations with Him, and rediscover the profound power of worship. I learned to stand unwaveringly on the truth found in His Word, make plans for a future that seemed uncertain, and, most importantly, trust God through it all.

I learned that letting friends into my life was not a sign of weakness but an essential source of strength, that helping others was a way to shift the focus from my pain to the needs of those around me, and that it was perfectly acceptable to grieve and cry. Through the process, I discovered the importance of tending to my own well-being by doing what I needed to do: addressing legal matters, eating healthily, and embracing regular exercise. Additionally, I found comfort in the beauty of travel, more mission trips, and the pursuit of lifelong dreams and passions that I had put on hold.

In the pages of this book, I aim to share these lessons and experiences to provide a guiding light for those traversing the challenging path of grief, whether that grief is born from the loss of a loved one, declining health, or a condition that sets you apart from others. This is a difficult season of life, but seasons change, and with hope, faith, and trust in Jesus, He will help you into your next season. Remember, you are going through it, and you won't be stuck there forever.

Chapter 1:

Regain Focus on God

The road through grief is one that each of us must traverse in our own time and at our own pace. There is no neatly defined timetable for the healing of a wounded heart. It's a journey that winds through valleys of sorrow and sometimes feels like an endless path of sadness. But one thing you must always remember is this: grief is a journey you are on; it is not a destination where you are destined to remain forever.

When my husband went to heaven, everything was a blur for a while. I got "widow brain," which is a term used to describe the fogginess and disconnect that can set in after the death of a spouse. It may not feel real at first, and the "widow brain" may be a protective mechanism of the human mind trying to protect itself from the potential stages of grief. It can impact almost every aspect of daily life and may be characterized by forgetfulness, extreme sadness, brain fog, irritability, fatigue or exhaustion, numbness, and nausea. The symptoms fade over time (usually two months to one year), but the grief will remain until you are able to work through it and move forward.

Around nine months after my beloved Carl passed away, I found myself at the lowest point of my grief journey. The weight of his absence bore down on me, and the future appeared shrouded in uncertainty. It was during this time that I had a pivotal encounter with a friend — a fellow widow who had been walking her own path of loss for about 12 years. She looked me in the eyes and said something that sent my heart into a tailspin: "It never gets any better."

As I was driving home from our lunch together, tears streamed down my face, and I cried out to God in desperation, "I can't do this! I need help!" It was a moment of raw vulnerability, a turning point in my grief journey. Subsequently, I discovered that God is always faithful, even in our darkest hours.

Before this pivotal encounter, I had already been aware of God's provision during my time of grieving. There were moments when I felt His presence in the most tangible ways. When my car's battery refused to start one day, leaving me bewildered and stranded, I turned to social media for help. I posted my dilemma on Facebook, and a good friend named Don responded with invaluable guidance: "Do you have AAA? If so, they'll come to your home and fix your battery right in your garage." That simple post triggered a memory buried deep within me—that Carl had signed us up for AAA the spring before he passed away. I hadn't remembered and certainly didn't know how it worked, as I had never used it before.

Another instance of God's divine care manifested when my mailbox was struck by a vehicle, leaving it damaged. I had plans to address the issue, but fate had different plans, and my mailbox was struck again—this time almost completely demolished. I emailed my neighbors, detailing the situation and urging them to remain vigilant, as I couldn't be certain if the damage was accidental or intentional. With vandalism a potential concern, I wanted my neighbors to be aware. Then, on the eve of the handyman's scheduled visit, I made a remarkable discovery: my mailbox had been not only replaced but also meticulously repaired, all anonymously. It was a gift from God, a poignant reminder that even amid profound loss, He was watching over me and providing in ways I could never have foreseen.

These moments, these acts of divine grace, were a testament to the unwavering love of our Heavenly Father. In the darkest hours of my grief, I learned that when we cry out for help, God is always ready to answer our prayers, often in ways that are both unexpected and profoundly touching.

My pastor and dear friend, Bill Cordrey, came over to counsel me the day after that devastating conversation with a fellow widow. Her words echoed in my mind: "It never gets any better." It was a statement that had cast a shadow over my already heavy heart. Bill, a skilled counselor, knew just what to say. He began by assuring me, "Pat, she was wrong. It does get better, and it definitely will for you."

Bill's counseling was personalized to fit my unique situation. He acknowledged that the deep bonds Carl and I had formed over the years could not be unraveled quickly. But he also recognized that the healing process would be facilitated through God's Word and a focus on my interests and individual circumstances.

In those days, I had not only lost my beloved husband but also my sense of joy and my focus on Jesus. It's easy to become consumed by self-pity when grief takes hold, and isolation only exacerbated my feelings of loneliness. Carl had passed away just before the onset of the Covid-19 pandemic, which brought about a level of isolation I had never experienced before. With church and Sunday School moved online, the loneliness was palpable, and it became a breeding ground for depression and sorrow.

Bill asked me a question that shifted my perspective: "Pat, why did you and Carl travel so much?" I replied with a description of the sheer excitement and joy that came with exploring new places and experiencing new adventures. I commented on the 99 countries I had visited and expressed my love for adventure. Then Bill asked me what one great adventure I would like to go on. After thinking for a few seconds, I said, "Heaven." That's when Bill delivered a powerful revelation: "Pat, that's what Carl did. He went on the next great adventure."

Suddenly, it all made sense. Carl had embarked on a journey beyond this earthly realm—a grand adventure into heaven. Bill's words realigned my perspective and breathed new life into my faith. He shared a parable from **Matthew 13:44 (ESV)**: "*The kingdom of heaven is like treasure hidden in a field, which a man found and covered up. Then, in his joy, he goes and sells all that he has and buys that field.*"

Bill emphasized those three words—in his joy—and it resonated deep within my soul. I had that treasure—Jesus. However, amid my grief, I had temporarily lost my joy.

Bill proposed a plan that involved traveling to Oklahoma to visit Carl's grave. There, I would spend one to two days in conversation with the Lord, processing my questions and emotions. Afterward, I would visit a church altar near the cemetery to continue my time of prayer and listening to Jesus. Given the months of isolation, Bill believed that being surrounded by the love of friends and family in Oklahoma would provide much-needed comfort. However, he stressed that this should come only after my time of reflection and prayer at Carl's grave.

When Bill left that evening, I found myself walking around my house, singing the words, "Christ is all I need…all that I need." That single counseling session was a turning point—a lifeline that helped me find my way back to a place of spiritual and emotional restoration.

In preparation for my trip, I penned several pages of questions, all directed to God. This practice was not new to me; I had often used journals or spiral notebooks to write out questions I wanted God to answer. As I immersed myself in God's Word, the Holy Spirit gently revealed the answers, often through specific Bible verses that I would diligently record in my notebook.

The trip to Oklahoma took place the following month, and by the time I arrived, God had already revealed the answers to nearly all of my questions. I followed Bill's plan meticulously, spending two days at Carl's grave and at the church altar near the cemetery where his Oklahoma funeral had been held. It was an intimate and precious time with Jesus.

My journey continued as I spent the first three nights with Gayle and Bob. Gayle had been my college roommate for four years, and she and Bob resided in Duncan, Oklahoma, near Marlow, where the cemetery is located. Their kindness and hospitality touched my heart. After that, I stayed with Earl and Nancy for three nights in Weatherford, Oklahoma. They had been our best friends during our time at Southwestern Baptist Theological Seminary in Fort Worth. Nancy surprised me with letters, cards, books, and gifts from widows in their church — thoughtful gestures that left me deeply moved. These ladies had written them for me at Nancy's request. It was thoughtful and kind for each of these ladies, who had been widows for a long time, to take their time and share encouragement and scriptures with me. I was swallowed up with love by Earl and Nancy in addition to their church widows. We spent lots of time talking about so many things. I remember telling them about things I missed. One thing I shared was that even though Carl wasn't one to cook steaks on the grill very often, I wished I had someone to cook a ribeye steak on the grill for me. It just sounded fun, especially after months of isolation.

My journey led me to Edmond, Oklahoma, where I visited Mary Jane and Mike. Mary Jane was a dear friend of mine from my college days at the University of Oklahoma. When I arrived, her husband Mike was very kind and said for us girls to visit as he would fix dinner for us. He said he was cooking ribeye steaks on the grill. I felt the overwhelming goodness of God at that moment. My visit with them was very special. Mary Jane and I went back to Norman, Oklahoma, on Sunday and went to church at First Baptist Church of Norman, Oklahoma, where we had all attended during our college years and where I was married.

The next stop was Broken Arrow, Oklahoma, my hometown, where five of my siblings still reside. They embraced me with love, birthday gifts, and the precious gift of time together. I stayed with one sister for the first week and another for the second, and the love and support they showered upon me were immeasurable.

Through these moments, I realized how God had used Bill's wisdom and counsel to redirect my focus to Jesus. Then, He used my time in Oklahoma to refill my love tank after months of loneliness. What this means to you is that to successfully navigate the challenging path of grief, you must restore your focus on Jesus. Without this laser-like focus on Him, the journey through grief can become a disorienting struggle, making it difficult to find your way. Jesus is the source of love and joy; you need Him now more than ever.

Perhaps as you read this book, you find yourself in a place where you don't yet know Jesus on a personal level. If that is the case, let me encourage you to cry out to Him now. You might not fully comprehend everything about Him at this moment, but if you sincerely cry out to Him and seek after Him, He will answer you. He will reveal things that you could never have seen on your own to you.

Right now, in this very moment, you can invite Him into your life. You can choose to follow Him for the rest of your life. In Jesus, you will discover hope, peace, and joy, even amid grief. You need Him, and He is always ready to meet you where you are.

Chapter 2:

Talk to God

Grief is a journey that often feels like a lonely road, and in the depths of your sorrow, it can be difficult to find comfort and understanding. In times of loss, it's natural to question the very foundations of your faith and to wrestle with feelings of anger, blame, and confusion. When a loved one is taken from you, it's all too easy to ask, "Why, God? Why did you allow this to happen?" It's a question that can weigh heavily on your heart.

In the midst of your grief, you may find it hard to approach God. You may hesitate to talk to Him, fearing that your emotions will spill out in ways that seem disrespectful or unfaithful. However, it's essential to understand that God is not a distant, unfeeling deity. He is a big God who can handle your anger, blame, and questions. Expressing your emotions isn't an act of excessive emotionality; it's a sincere cry to God, laying bare your complete self. He wants you to come to Him with your pain and your doubts, just as you are.

During my own journey through grief, I also faced a multitude of questions. I grappled with the "whys" and "what ifs" that seemed to have no end. Like you, I needed answers, and so I turned to God in prayer. I made a list of questions for Him to answer. It was a long list of about 20 questions tailored to my situation and required direct answers. For example, I asked Him, "Who will I travel with now?" and "What should I do now that I retired to be with and care for Carl and he isn't here?" "Should I go back to work?" "What good can You bring out of this situation?" "Should I date anyone else or stay single?" Although my questions were very specific to my situation, here are some questions you might ask:

- Why did You take my loved one from me?
- Couldn't You have intervened and spared their life?
- What purpose could possibly be served by this loss?
- Did I do something to deserve this pain?
- How can I find meaning in this suffering?
- Where are You in all of this?

As I prayed and read His Word, I discovered that God is not offended by our questions. He invites us to ask and seek understanding, even when our hearts are heavy with sorrow. In fact, the Bible is full of examples of people who questioned God in times of despair—Job, David, and even Jesus on the cross. They cried out, and God heard them.

God began to reveal answers to my questions through the Holy Spirit speaking to my heart and His Word, giving specific verses. It was not always an immediate or miraculous experience, but it was a gradual unfolding of understanding as I persistently sought Him. The clarity of these answers became evident, with most stemming directly from Scripture as I delved into daily Bible readings during my in-depth study. Prayer is not you doing all the talking; it is hearing from Him through His Word, which is the primary way He speaks to you.

God wanted me to continue serving Him with mission trips, learning more Spanish, and joining a vacation club to have opportunities to travel with others. To the question of dating, He gave me three verses on that question:

Matthew 6:33-34 (NIV): *"But seek first his kingdom and his righteousness, and all these things will be given to you as well.*

Therefore do not worry about tomorrow, for tomorrow will worry about itself. Each day has enough trouble of its own."

Matthew 7:7-8 (NIV): *"Ask and it will be given to you; seek and you will find; knock and the door will be opened to you. For everyone who asks receives; the one who seeks finds, and to the one who knocks, the door will be opened."*

Isaiah 54:4-5 (NIV): *"Do not be afraid; you will not be put to shame. Do not fear disgrace; you will not be humiliated. You will forget the shame of your youth and remember no more the reproach of your widowhood. For your Maker is your husband – the Lord Almighty is his name – the Holy One of Israel is your Redeemer; he is called the God of all the earth."*

I thought that was clear: Seek Him first, He hears and provides, don't worry about the future or be afraid, and He will be my Husband.

To the question of going back to work, He showed **me Isaiah 40:1-2 (NIV)**:

"Comfort, comfort my people, says your God. Speak tenderly to Jerusalem, and proclaim to her that her hard service has been completed, that her sin has been paid for, that she has received from the Lord's hand double for all her sins."

It was specifically saying to me that my hard work was over, which meant my regular days of serving in a medical office.

Another question He gave an extensive answer to was, "When I get lonely, sad, grieving, discouraged, or frustrated, how can I let it go more easily and get back to where I should be?" These verses were His answer:

- **Psalm 25:15 (NIV)**: *"My eyes are ever on the Lord, for only he will release my feet from the snare."*

- **Psalm 30:11-12 (NIV)**: *"You turned my wailing into dancing; you removed my sackcloth and clothed me with joy, that my heart may sing your praises and not be silent. Lord my God, I will praise you forever."*

- **Psalm 31:7-8 (NIV)**: *"I will be glad and rejoice in your love, for you saw my affliction and knew the anguish of my soul. You have not given me into the hands of the enemy but have set my feet in a spacious place."*

- **Psalm 31:24 (NIV)**: *"Be strong and take heart, all you who hope in the Lord."*

- **Psalm 119:76 (NIV)**: *"May your unfailing love be my comfort, according to your promise to your servant."*

- **Psalm 116:7-9 (NIV)**: *"Return to your rest, my soul, for the Lord has been good to you. For you, Lord, have delivered me from death, my eyes from tears, my feet from stumbling, that I may walk before the Lord in the land of the living."*

Just as I left blank lines after each question in my journal, and God unveiled the answers to me through His Word or through the guidance of the Holy Spirit, He will do the same for you. His Word is there for you; reading it is your way of knowing what He thinks on any topic. Prayer isn't just a monologue; it's a dialogue. It's not solely about us doing all the talking but also about listening to Him through His Word. This is the primary channel through which He chooses to communicate with us.

The answers I received often came straight out of my daily quiet time of reading the Bible and praying. When a verse seemed to jump out at me, I wrote it down alongside my questions. I discovered that God's Word is a wellspring of comfort, guidance, and hope in times of grief. My prayer time was not just a series of questions that needed to be answered. It was access to the throneroom of God, and His presence flooded my heart with peace and love.

The Bible reminds us that God is close to the brokenhearted (Psalm 34:18) and that He cares for us (1 Peter 5:7). It tells us that even though we may walk through the valley of the shadow of death, we need not fear, for God is with us (Psalm 23:4). His promises are a source of strength and assurance when we need it most.

One of the most renowned stories of suffering and loss in the Bible is that of Job. Job, a righteous and prosperous man, is struck by a series of unimaginable tragedies: he loses his wealth, health, and children. In the face of such profound suffering, Job questions the very nature of his existence and engages in a profound dialogue with God and his friends. Job's story reminds us that suffering is an inherent part of the human experience, irrespective of our righteousness. Through his trials, he questions why God allows such pain and loss to befall him. Job's journey illustrates the importance of confronting our suffering, questioning it, and seeking understanding, even when the answers seem elusive. Ultimately, Job's faith and resilience are rewarded, demonstrating that endurance in the face of adversity can lead to spiritual growth and restoration.

In the biblical narrative of 1 Samuel 1, we encounter the story of Hannah, a woman who struggled with the profound grief of infertility. Hannah's infertility was not merely a physical challenge; it was a deep emotional and spiritual burden. She longed for a child, a desire rooted in the cultural and societal expectations of her time but also in her heart's earnest yearning. Her grief was overwhelming, and her prayers fervent and tearful, and they reflected the depth of her pain. Hannah's raw and honest prayers demonstrate the importance of approaching God with complete transparency. She did not hide her anguish but poured out her soul before the Lord. You must know that it is okay to express your pain, doubts, and frustrations in prayer. God welcomes your vulnerability and offers comfort in your honesty. He appreciates your authentic prayers to Him for help.

Hannah's husband, Elkanah, offered emotional support during her grief. Also, after initially misunderstanding her anguish, the priest Eli eventually prayed for her. This emphasizes the significance of leaning on a supportive Christian community during times of grief. Sharing your burdens with fellow believers can provide comfort and strength. Maybe you need to get a dedicated prayer partner to help you through this difficult season. I did, and it has really helped me. She and I pray together each Tuesday morning at 7:00 A.M. You can ask a friend to call you each week and pray together over the phone.

Hannah's story reminds you that God's timing is not always aligned with your own. She patiently waited for God's intervention, and when it came, she recognized that her son, Samuel, was a gift from God with a unique purpose. Grief often comes with questions about why suffering occurs, but Hannah's faith in God's plan demonstrates that He can bring beauty from pain.

Even in her grief, Hannah continued to talk to God. She made a vow to dedicate her son to the Lord's service, a testament to her unwavering faith. You can learn that even in the midst of grief, you must talk to God.

Ultimately, Hannah's story teaches you about the possibility of hope and restoration through this trying time. After years of barrenness, she became a mother, and God blessed her with more children. Her story illustrates that grief is not the end but a part of a larger narrative of God's faithfulness and redemption.

In your grief, remember that it's okay to ask questions and to express your anger and doubts to God. He welcomes your honesty. Through your dialogue with Him, you will find the healing and understanding you seek and specific answers to your questions. Just as He comforted and guided me with answers to my questions, He will also speak to your heart, offering comfort and wisdom in the midst of your pain.

My challenge to you is to talk to God. Pour out your heart to Him, list your questions, and leave space for His answers not just in your journal but in your heart as well. Trust that, with time, you will find the peace that surpasses all understanding, even in the midst of grief. God is waiting, arms open wide, to walk this challenging journey with you.

Chapter 3:

Know and Stand on Truth

In the depths of grief, when sorrow engulfs your heart and darkness seems to shroud your soul, it is easy to lose your way. The journey through grief can be a winding and treacherous path that may leave you feeling lost, abandoned, and utterly alone. However, in the midst of this crushing sorrow, there is a guiding light, a beacon of hope that can illuminate even the darkest of moments. That light is the eternal truth found in God's Word.

The Bible is a source of immense comfort and wisdom for those who are grieving. It provides you with a solid foundation on which to stand when your world has crumbled around you. In this chapter, you will explore several key Bible verses that share profound truths about grief and how you can find peace, comfort, and strength in God's promises.

1. **Psalm 34:18 (NIV)**

"The Lord is close to the brokenhearted and saves those who are crushed in spirit."

During the depths of your grief, it's not uncommon to feel that God is distant, as if He has abandoned you in your pain. However, this verse serves as a comforting reminder that, in reality, God draws near to you when your heart is broken. He isn't a distant observer of your suffering but a compassionate presence in your moments of pain. When the weight of grief crushes you, God is there to rescue you, lift you up, and mend your shattered spirit. I recall speaking to God in the first week after Carl's passing, saying, "It's just You and me again." I had been married at the age of 22, so it hadn't been just God and me for 41 years. I recollected how close He was to me in my teens and longed for that intimate connection once more. Thankfully, I am even closer to Him now. In fact, He is my life. You can have that too.

2. 2 Corinthians 1:3-4 (NIV)

"Praise be to the God and Father of our Lord Jesus Christ, the Father of compassion and the God of all comfort, who comforts us in all our troubles so that we can comfort those in any trouble with the comfort we ourselves receive from God."

Grief is not a road you travel alone. God, the Father of compassion, walks beside you, offering comfort and solace in your times of trouble. His comfort is not just for your benefit; it equips you to be a source of comfort to others who are grieving. As you receive God's comfort, you become a conduit of His love and compassion, extending hope to those who are hurting.

3. **Isaiah 43:2 (NIV)**

"When you pass through the waters, I will be with you, and when you pass through the rivers, they will not sweep over you. When you walk through the fire, you will not be burned; the flames will not set you ablaze."

Grief often feels like an overwhelming flood, threatening to drown you in despair. But this verse reminds you that even in the midst of life's most trying circumstances, God promises to be with you. He will not allow the waters to overwhelm you nor the fires to consume you. His presence is your lifeline, ensuring that you emerge from grief stronger and more resilient than before.

4. **Romans 8:28 (NIV)**

"And we know that in all things God works for the good of those who love him, who have been called according to his purpose."

Grief can leave you questioning the purpose and meaning of your suffering. But this verse reassures you that God is at work, even in your pain, weaving together a tapestry of good from the threads of your sorrow. Nothing is wasted in God's economy, and He can use even the most painful experiences to fulfill His purposes in your life. He is faithful to bring good out of the rough times in your life.

5. **Revelation 21:4 (NIV)**

"He will wipe every tear from their eyes. There will be no more death or mourning or crying or pain, for the old order of things has passed away."

Ultimately, your hope as a believer in Jesus is not just in the comfort God offers you in your grief but in the promise of a future where grief will no longer exist. In the new heaven and new earth, God will wipe away every tear, and sorrow will be no more. This eternal perspective reminds you that your present suffering is temporary, and a glorious, grief-free future awaits you in God's presence if you belong to His family.

6. **Matthew 5:4 (NIV)**

"Blessed are those who mourn, for they will be comforted."

In His famous Sermon on the Mount, Jesus spoke directly to the hearts of those who are grieving. He assured you that you are blessed and promised that you will be comforted. This beatitude reminds you that even in your sorrow, God's blessings and comfort are available to you.

7. **Psalm 42:11 (NIV)**

"Why, my soul, are you downcast? Why so disturbed within me? Put your hope in God, for I will yet praise him, my Savior and my God."

Grief can often bring a profound sense of despair, but this verse encourages you to turn your gaze toward God. It reminds you that you can put your hope in Him even in the depths of sorrow. Your grief need not define you; your hope in God is your anchor through the storm.

8. **1 Peter 5:7 (NIV)**

"Cast all your anxiety on Him because He cares for you."

The burden of grief can be heavy, but you are not meant to carry it alone. God invites you to cast all your anxiety, including your sorrow, upon Him because He deeply cares for you. In surrendering your pain to Him, you find relief and rest for your weary soul.

9. Lamentations 3:22-23 (NIV)

"Because of the Lord's great love we are not consumed, for his compassions never fail. They are new every morning; great is your faithfulness."

Grief can feel all-consuming, but these verses remind you that God's love and compassion are boundless and unchanging. His faithfulness is unwavering, and each new day brings a fresh outpouring of His compassion to sustain you.

10. 2 Corinthians 4:17-18 (NIV)

"For our light and momentary troubles are achieving for us an eternal glory that far outweighs them all. So we fix our eyes not on what is seen, but on what is unseen since what is seen is temporary, but what is unseen is eternal."

Amid grief, it's easy to become fixated on your immediate pain and suffering. However, these verses remind you to focus on the eternal perspective. No matter how heavy, your present troubles are temporary, but the glory that awaits you in eternity far surpasses them. This perspective gives you the strength to endure and the hope to persevere.

11. **Psalm 30:5 (NIV)**

"For his anger lasts only a moment, but his favor lasts a lifetime; weeping may stay for the night, but rejoicing comes in the morning."

Sadness often feels like an unending night, but this verse assures you that joy will come in the morning. God's favor and grace endure, and He promises to turn your mourning into dancing.

12. **John 14:27 (NIV)**

"Peace I leave with you; my peace I give you. I do not give to you as the world gives. Do not let your hearts be troubled and do not be afraid."

Amidst the turmoil of grief, Jesus offers you His peace that surpasses understanding. It is a peace that calms troubled hearts and banishes fear. In Christ, you find a refuge of tranquility even amid life's greatest storms.

13. **Psalm 56:8 (NIV)**

"You keep track of all my sorrows. You have collected all my tears in your bottle. You have recorded each one in your book."

God not only sees your tears but treasures them. He keeps a record of your sorrows, a testament to His deep concern for your pain. Your tears are not in vain; they are precious to Him.

14. **1 Thessalonians 4:13-14 (NIV)**

"Brothers and sisters, we do not want you to be uninformed about those who sleep in death so that you do not grieve like the rest of mankind, who have no hope. For we believe that Jesus died and rose again, and so we believe that God will bring with Jesus those who have fallen asleep in him."

In times of grief, you may be tempted to grieve like those who have no hope. But as a follower of Jesus, you have a profound hope in the resurrection. Your grief is not the end; it is a temporary separation from your loved ones who have fallen asleep in Christ. You can look forward to a glorious reunion in His presence.

15. **Psalm 30:11-12 (NIV)**

"You turned my wailing into dancing; you removed my sackcloth and clothed me with joy, that my heart may sing your praises and not be silent. Lord my God, I will praise you forever."

God is the ultimate orchestrator of transformation in your grief. He turns your mourning into dancing, your sorrow into joy. Your journey through grief ultimately becomes a path of praise as you experience the transformative power of God's love.

My dear friend Christie introduced me to The Bible Recap, an online Bible reading plan that takes you on a chronological journey through God's Word every year when paired with The Bible App. The added commentary on each reading made it even more enticing. As someone who has always had an affinity for audio learning, I immediately resonated with this approach. In fact, I delved into it so wholeheartedly that over the past two years, I've immersed myself in the entire Bible 2.5 times annually.

I've discovered a profound joy in listening to God's Word as I go about my daily activities—whether it's my daily walk through the neighborhood, the process of getting dressed, tending to household chores, preparing meals, or even during my driving time to pick up my grandchildren. This practice has evolved into a wellspring of hope and tranquility in my life as I get to hear from Him each and every day. There's something truly special about experiencing His truth as it unfolds chronologically through Scripture.

Before embracing The Bible Recap, I delved into many workbook-style Bible studies by authors like Beth Moore and Priscilla Shirer. These studies are immersive, delving deeply into God's Word, dissecting it with numerous thought-provoking questions, and providing accompanying Scriptures to illuminate the true essence of the passages. They go further by offering practical applications to integrate into your life. These studies can take various forms, focusing on specific topics or dedicated to exploring particular books of the Bible.

My extensive history of diligently studying God's Word and committing substantial portions of it to memory lays the groundwork for the Holy Spirit to work through these verses, offering solace and guidance during moments of despair. The verses surface in my mind, acting as steadfast sustenance through the trials and tribulations. They have served me well and can undoubtedly do the same for you.

Moreover, I have the privilege of teaching a ladies' Sunday school class and speaking at women's ministry events. These endeavors demand continuous study and a fresh word from God on each occasion. His desire for us to immerse ourselves in His Word is abundantly clear. It equips us to navigate the trials and temptations of life, reassuring us that He is good all the time.

As you journey through the wilderness of grief, you must hold fast to these truths from God's Word. They are the solid ground on which you can stand when everything else is shaking. God is with you in your pain, offering comfort, purpose, and the hope of a brighter tomorrow. Knowing and standing on these truths will give you the strength to persevere and the courage to comfort others who walk the same path of grief.

My challenge to you is to memorize these truths from God's Word that are listed in this chapter. Also, you must embark on a daily Bible reading plan that fits your lifestyle and available time. It will be your lifeline for hearing from God each day. You should also join a group for Bible study. This can be a Sunday school class, small group, or online group.

Chapter 4:

Worship

In the heart of your grief journey, worship may initially seem incongruent. You might find it hard to lift your voice in praise, to sing the songs of faith, or to utter words of adoration when your heart is heavy with sorrow. Grief can shroud your spirit, casting a veil over the vibrant connection you once had with God. Yet, it is in these very moments of despair that worship can be a balm for your aching soul.

Worship, my dear reader, is not solely reserved for moments of celebration and joy. It is, in fact, most powerful in the midst of your grief. The reason lies in the resurrection of our Lord and Savior, Jesus Christ. He conquered death, and in doing so, He paved the way for you to worship even when your heart is heavy and your eyes are clouded with tears.

Grief has a way of casting a heavy shadow over our lives, dimming even the brightest corners of our hearts. In the wake of a severe loss, many of us find ourselves struggling to worship God. It's as if our voices have been stolen by sorrow, and the songs of praise that once flowed freely from our lips are now silenced. My father once told me that it took him weeks before he could sing again after my mother's death. It's a sentiment shared by countless others who have walked the path of grief. My own story is that even though I sang songs it was inauthentic worship. I wasn't worshiping in my heart. It was not until I repented of this false worship and truly began worshiping God again that I felt completely whole. When my spirit joined with His Spirit, I was once again honestly adoring Him and praising Him.

Let's begin our exploration of worship by turning to **Hebrews 13:15-16 (ESV):**

"Through him then let us continually offer up a sacrifice of praise to God, that is, the fruit of lips that acknowledge his name. Do not neglect to do good and to share what you have, for such sacrifices are pleasing to God."

This verse reminds you that your worship is a sacrifice to God, one that involves the fruit of your lips acknowledging His name. Even in your sorrow, you can offer Him this sacrifice, knowing that it is pleasing to Him. There is something truly remarkable that happens when we choose to worship despite our grief. It's as if, in the act of lifting our voices and acknowledging God's name, our hearts begin to shift. Worship becomes a catalyst for healing. As we sing or speak words of praise, the truth of God's love, compassion, and faithfulness begins to penetrate our grief-stricken souls. Slowly but surely, worship becomes an authentic and genuine outpouring of our hearts. The Bible offers guidance and comfort to those who find it difficult to worship in the midst of grief:

Psalm 42:11 (NIV): *"Why, my soul, are you downcast? Why so disturbed within me? Put your hope in God, for I will yet praise him, my Savior and my God."* - Even in the depths of sorrow, the psalmist recognizes the importance of putting hope in God and praising Him.

Psalm 34:18 (NIV): *"The Lord is close to the brokenhearted and saves those who are crushed in spirit."* - In your brokenness, God draws near. Worship can be a bridge that connects you to His comforting presence.

Psalm 30:11-12 (NIV): *"You turned my wailing into dancing; you removed my sackcloth and clothed me with joy, that my heart may sing your praises and not be silent. Lord my God, I will praise you forever."* - This passage reminds you that God can transform your mourning into dancing and your silence into praise.

Isaiah 61:3 (NIV): *"...and provide for those who grieve in Zion – to bestow on them a crown of beauty instead of ashes, the oil of joy instead of mourning, and a garment of praise instead of a spirit of despair."* - God offers you a "garment of praise" even in your moments of despair.

Worship is not just an expression of joy; it's a lifeline in the midst of grief. It's a way to connect with God, to release your pain, and to receive His healing touch. When you offer your sacrifice of praise, you open your heart to the possibility of transformation. Even when it feels like a distant melody, remember that worship has the power to mend the broken places within you and draw you closer to the One who can truly heal your soul. In times of grief, may you find the strength to lift your voice and declare the goodness of God, for He is with you, even in the valley of sorrow.

Worship extends far beyond singing praise songs. I distinctly recall sitting in my first and second years of medical school, utterly awestruck by the intricate workings of the human body. I couldn't help but marvel at the creativity and magnificence of God, the Designer behind every intricate detail. Each time I learned something new about His design,

I eagerly anticipated going home to share this glimpse of God's handiwork with others.

True worship involves not just acknowledging the wonders of the human body but also recognizing God's hand in the grand design of the universe. It's about understanding how the Earth spins on its axis, perfectly positioned relative to the sun, ensuring that we neither burn up nor freeze. It's those moments when I see God's hand at work in a situation, orchestrated for my good and His glory, that I can't help but look up to the heavens and say, "I know that was You."

Worship is the spontaneous outburst of praise when God protects me or answers a specific prayer. It's those sleepless nights when I find myself lying awake for hours, overwhelmed with gratitude and praise to God. This often occurs when I'm overjoyed, like the time He entrusted me with the opportunity to individually share the gospel with 41 different people who accepted Jesus as their Savior during my last mission trip to Peru. I vividly remember one instance when I heard that 25 people had prayed to accept Christ on the first day of my trip to Paraguay. That night, I spent over two hours worshiping Him, my heart overflowing with thankfulness.

Additionally, worship can manifest itself through the physical—like my heart rate, as measured by my Fitbit, skyrocketing during 75 minutes of engaging in drive-through prayer. As I wave at people and pray for them, Jesus fills me with boundless joy.

Worship is not confined to grand gestures or public performances. It's also the simple act of preparing a song to sing in a worship service but finding so much delight in singing it at home, with Him as my only Audience. While I sing to Him, my heart rate rises for hours, even though I'm not exercising, simply because I sense His presence.

Worship is in the gaze upon God's creation, whether it's the vast ocean from the shoreline or the vibrant fish encountered while snorkeling. It's the thrill of witnessing His majesty and creativity. It's the exuberant "Praise the Lord!" that spontaneously escapes my lips when I hear about how He has worked in someone's life. It's the sheer wonder that fills my heart as I watch the birth of a baby or peer into a beating heart during surgery, with the thought, "You designed this, and it is so good."

Worship also flows from the affectionate embrace of a grandchild or friend, so enveloping that it feels as though

God Himself is hugging me through them. In those moments, I can't help but turn my face upward and whisper, "Thank You." Worship is the humble act of falling to my knees and lifting my hands in gratitude for who He is. It's seeing a rainbow and being moved to thank Him for His promises. It's recognizing His spectacular nature and struggling to find the words to express that overwhelming feeling. Worship, in essence, encompasses every facet of life and every moment in which we encounter the divine presence of God.

The Bible is rich with verses that emphasize the importance of worship in our lives, especially during times of grief. Consider the example of Job, a man who experienced immense suffering. In the face of his overwhelming grief, he chose to worship God. Job 1:20-21 (NIV) tells us, *"At this, Job got up and tore his robe and shaved his head. Then he fell to the ground in worship and said: 'Naked I came from my mother's womb, and naked I will depart. The Lord gave and the Lord has taken away; may the name of the Lord be praised.'"*

Job's response to tragedy was worship. He didn't understand why he was enduring such pain, but he knew that God was worthy of his worship, even in grief. Job's faith in God's character allowed him to find comfort and express his adoration in the darkest of times.

Consider the example of David, the renowned psalmist and King of Israel. He experienced profound grief throughout his life, yet he turned to worship in the midst of his trials. When his child fell gravely ill, David fasted and lay on the ground in prayer. However, when the child died, his servants were amazed at his response. Instead of descending further into despair, David arose, washed, and anointed himself. He went into the house of the Lord and worshiped, understanding that though the child could not return to him, he would go to the child (2 Samuel 12:19-23, ESV).

In the New Testament, in the Hall of Faith, found in Hebrews chapter 11, there's a remarkable example of worship amid grief. In verse 20, we read about Isaac blessing Jacob and Esau, anticipating his own death. **Hebrews 11:20 (ESV)** states, "*By faith Isaac invoked future blessings on Jacob and Esau.*" Isaac's act of invoking blessings was an act of worship. Even as he faced his impending death, he demonstrated unwavering faith and trust in God, acknowledging His sovereignty. He blessed his sons, entrusting their futures to God. This act of worship revealed his deep faith in God's plan, even during his own time of grief and uncertainty.

In the Gospel of John, we find the account of Martha and Mary grieving the death of their brother, Lazarus. Despite their profound sorrow, they worshiped Jesus when He arrived. Martha expressed her faith in Jesus, saying, "I believe that you are the Christ, the Son of God" (John 11:27, ESV), and Mary fell at His feet in worship (John 11:32). Their worship, even in the face of death, was met with the miracle of Lazarus' resurrection.

In Acts 16, we find Paul and Silas imprisoned and in physical pain. Despite their dire circumstances, they prayed and sang hymns to God, turning their confinement into an opportunity for worship. Their worship was so powerful that it led to a miraculous earthquake and the salvation of the jailer and his household.

The prophet Jeremiah, often called the "weeping prophet," expressed his grief and lament in the book of Lamentations. Yet, even in the midst of his sorrow, he turns to God in worship, recognizing God's faithfulness (Lamentations 3:22-23)

Hannah, who experienced infertility and deep sorrow, worshiped the Lord in her grief. She prayed fervently for a child, and when God answered her prayer with the birth of

Samuel, she composed a heartfelt prayer of thanksgiving and worship (1 Samuel 1:10-20).

The lesson here is clear: Worship is not reserved for the sunny days of life but is a lifeline to hold onto when the storms of grief threaten to consume you. God deserves your worship in every circumstance, even in sadness. In your darkest hours, when it feels as if your world is crumbling, remember that worship can be a source of strength, a channel through which God's comfort flows into your life. These examples from the Bible illustrate the profound connection between worship and grief. In the most challenging moments of life, these individuals turned to God in worship, finding comfort, strength, and even miracles in their acts of adoration. This demonstrates that worship can be a source of comfort and healing, even in the darkest times.

So, I urge you, my friend, not to let grief silence your worship. Lift your voice, sing your songs, and utter your words of adoration, even when tears are streaming down your face. As you do, you'll find that worship can transform your grief into an offering of praise, bringing comfort and peace to your troubled heart. So, I challenge you to turn your radio on to the most uplifting worship music and sing along with a loud voice. You will experience the transforming power of worship.

Chapter 5:

Do for Others

In the depths of grief, it's all too easy to become ensnared by the suffocating grip of sorrow. The weight of loss can press down upon your heart, leaving you feeling isolated and consumed by your own pain. Yet, amid the darkness, there is a ray of light, a path toward healing that can lead you out of the shadows: the simple act of doing for others.

Grief has a way of making you feel like the world revolves around your sorrow as if it's the only thing that matters. However, in these moments, you can find comfort and purpose by shifting your focus from yourself to others. When you choose to think of those who are hurting or less fortunate than you, something remarkable happens—the weight of your grief begins to lift, and your own sorrows seem to dim.

The act of helping others in need is like a balm for the soul. It takes your attention off your pain and redirects it toward someone else's suffering. Suddenly, your burdens don't feel quite as heavy when you are carrying them alongside another person in need. In reaching out to those who are hurting, you discover that your capacity for compassion is boundless, even in your own time of sorrow.

When you plan to do things for others, it's not just an altruistic endeavor; it's a source of joy and healing for yourself. There is a profound sense of fulfillment that comes from knowing you've made a positive impact on someone else's life, even in the midst of your own struggles. It's a reminder that, despite your pain, you still have the power to bring the love of Jesus to someone who really needs it and is frequently worse off than you.

My personal journey of offering a helping hand to those in need has encompassed not only those facing greater challenges but also those who have recently embarked on their own path of grief. My qualification to provide support to those in the throes of grief was not a path I chose. It was thrust upon me. However, it's a journey I've navigated successfully, and it has equipped me to assist others who find themselves on a similar road.

I hope my experiences can serve as a guiding light for you as you journey through your trials. Over time, I've reached out to friends who were grappling with the weight of grief, sharing with them the insights and wisdom that are detailed in this book. My aim is to provide a source of solace and encouragement for those in need, drawing from the lessons I've learned along the way.

The Bible offers guidance and encouragement on the importance of doing for others, especially in times of grief:

Galatians 6:2 (NIV): *"Carry each other's burdens, and in this way, you will fulfill the law of Christ."* - Helping others with their burdens can alleviate the weight of your own.

Matthew 25:35-36 (NIV): *"For I was hungry and you gave me something to eat, I was thirsty and you gave me something to drink, I was a stranger and you invited me in, I needed clothes and you clothed me, I was sick and you looked after me, I was in prison and you came to visit me."* - Serving others is as if you are serving Christ Himself.

Philippians 2:4 (NIV): *"Each of you should look not only to your own interests but also to the interests of others."* - Grief can isolate us, but serving others bridges the gap.

Acts 20:35 (NIV): *"It is more blessed to give than to receive."* - The act of giving and helping others brings blessings and joy even in your own time of need.

In your journey through grief, consider the transformative power of doing for others. Whether it's volunteering, reaching out to a friend in need, or simply performing acts of kindness, these acts of selflessness can lift the weight of grief from your shoulders. They shine a light into the darkest corners of your heart, revealing that, even in your sorrow, you have the capacity to bring hope, love, and joy to those around you.

In the book of Genesis, Joseph experienced significant trials and grief, including being sold into slavery by his brothers and later being falsely accused and imprisoned in Egypt. Despite his own suffering, Joseph served others in prison by interpreting dreams for fellow inmates. His ability to use his gifts to help others eventually led to his release and an elevated position in Egypt (Genesis 40-41).

Ruth's story in the Old Testament is one of loss and grief, having lost her husband. She chose to serve her grieving mother-in-law, Naomi, rather than abandon her. Ruth's selfless commitment and dedication to Naomi eventually led to her marriage to Boaz and played a pivotal role in the lineage of King David (Ruth 1-4).

In the book of Acts, we encounter the story of Dorcas, a woman known for her acts of charity and service to the poor. When she died, her community mourned her deeply. The disciples in Joppa sent for Peter, who prayed over her, and she was brought back to life. Her service to others left a lasting impact on her community (Acts 9:36-42).

These examples demonstrate the transformative power of serving others in the midst of grief. Despite their own hardships, these individuals extended compassion and care to those in need, leaving a profound mark on their communities and the biblical narrative.

I made a deliberate choice to restart mission trips and also dedicated my time to volunteering at a cooperative ministry, specifically in the clothing closet. This was particularly meaningful because many of the patrons primarily spoke Spanish, offering me an opportunity to connect on a more personal level with them while using the Spanish I had been studying.

My reentry into various roles within the church community, including women's ministry leadership and teaching a ladies' Sunday school class, provided me with avenues to serve others. Within these roles, I took on responsibilities such as coordinating meal trains, preparing and delivering meals, and visiting members who were sick. Additionally, I extended a helping hand to those in need, assisting with transportation and offering financial support during challenging times. Another significant contribution I made was in organizing and staffing the drive-through prayer initiative, which has not only served our local community but has also been a valuable outreach effort for our church. Engaging in the necessary preparations for these responsibilities allowed me to satisfy my passion for studying, planning, and orchestrating various tasks while simultaneously redirecting my focus towards helping others.

When I retired, my initial plans centered around caring for Carl and traveling alongside him, leaving little room for a vision of retirement that didn't include him. Consequently, I found myself reevaluating how I would spend my time, and reaching out to assist others emerged as a fulfilling and meaningful use of my newfound free time.

I challenge you to choose to extend your hand, and you'll find that, in helping others, you help yourself as well. The world becomes a bit brighter, your pain a bit lighter, and your heart a bit fuller. In the act of doing for others, you'll discover a powerful antidote to grief — one that offers healing and a profound sense of purpose and connection to God and the world around you. So, can I sign you up to go with me on my next mission trip to Africa or South America to serve the poor and unreached people of these areas? If so, visit my website at www.for-gods-glory.com. I can guarantee you will feel the transforming power of God by serving others less fortunate than you.

Chapter 6:

Let Your Friends Help

Our friends often become unsung heroes who stand by our side in times of grief, extending their love, support, and understanding. This chapter serves as a tribute to those friends who step forward, offering their helping hands and loving hearts, and as an invitation for you to embrace their kindness as a source of healing and strength.

The simplicity of a sympathy card can bring immeasurable comfort. I still remember when a dear friend sent me a card filled with Scriptures about hope following the loss of another family member. Her handwritten verses provided a tremendous source of hope and strength for my aching soul. Proverbs 12:25 (NIV) highlights the significance of thoughtful words: "Anxiety weighs down the heart, but a kind word cheers it up." So, as you navigate your grief journey, be open to the kind words and gestures of your friends, for they have the power to uplift your spirits and brighten your path.

Friends who extend invitations for outings or trips are offering more than just an opportunity – they're providing an escape from isolation. It's crucial to accept these invitations whenever possible. If a conflict arises, graciously accept a rain check and try to reschedule. My friends didn't just invite me to join them on trips or dining out. They also extended their assistance to practical tasks, which, in the long run, proved to be invaluable. For instance, in a recent incident where my TV had sound but wouldn't display a picture, my daughter and son-in-law provided advice to unplug it, leave it off for a few minutes, then plug it back in and turn it on. I followed their suggestion twice, but it didn't resolve the issue. In my moment of need, I reached out to my friend Bill, who promptly searched the internet and found a video addressing the specific problem. After watching the video, the solution became clear: I needed to update the TV's software, and upon restarting it, the TV worked perfectly. Bill's quick thinking and resourcefulness were truly a blessing during that time.

Ecclesiastes 4:9-10 (NIV) emphasizes the strength of companionship: *"Two are better than one because they have a* *good return for their labor: If either of them falls down, one can help the other up."* Embrace these invitations to lean on the strength of friendship and share life's joys, even amidst grief.

A friend who becomes your movie buddy is a testament to the healing power of shared experiences. My friend, Amy, offered to accompany me to movies regularly, ensuring that I didn't have to sit alone or leave a dark theater by myself. If you don't already have a movie buddy (or a concert buddy), consider taking the initiative. Reach out and see if a friend would be willing to attend a sporting event, concert, or movie with you. I've attended the SEC Championship football game with friends Christie and David and the Mercy Me, Toby Mac, and Zach Williams concert with Lewann and Tina. Nan has invited me to the Atlanta Symphony several times, and we have shared meals out. It's not about whether it's your favorite team or concert type. It's about sharing time with loving friends. Your movie buddy serves as a reminder that you're not alone in facing life's challenges, big or small.

At times, well-meaning friends who wish to offer their support may appreciate a bit of direction on how best to assist you. In some instances, you might need to take the initiative and invite them to join you for a theatrical play or concert. For instance, I hold two season tickets to the local

Aurora Theater, and I've chosen to retain both tickets so that I can share the experience with a different friend for each performance.

These friends often include individuals who are also single or widows, and both they and I find comfort in the companionship that usually involves a delightful dinner before the show. This not only enhances our bond but also creates cherished memories of shared experiences.

Isaiah 41:10 (NIV) provides assurance: *"So do not fear, for I am with you; do not be dismayed, for I am your God. I will strengthen you and help you; I will uphold you with my righteous right hand."* Acts of connection, like Nancy connecting me with widows from her church, who reached out with letters, cards, and grief-related books, illustrate the care of friends in a Christian community. **Romans 12:15 (NIV)** encourages us: *"Rejoice with those who rejoice; mourn with those who mourn."* Your friends, both old and new, are walking this journey alongside you, sharing in your moments of joy and sorrow.

Support can manifest in various ways, such as counseling from Bill, a vacation invitation from Bill and Piper, shared meals, and Dianne's offer to be a prayer partner. **Proverbs 27:9 (NIV)** speaks to the value of heartfelt advice from a friend: "*Perfume and incense bring joy to the heart, and the pleasantness of a friend springs from their heartfelt advice.*" Welcome your friends' counsel and prayers, as their wisdom and companionship are precious gifts during your grief journey.

I'll never forget the day Carl passed into heaven, when my dear friends, Kathy R., Kathy C., and Dianne, showed up at my house to take me to lunch. They had been friends for years and spent hours with me that day. Since then, we've shared trips and cherished moments of friendship until Kathy R. also joined Carl in heaven. Now, Dianne and Kathy C. continue to travel with me, and we often dine out together, encouraging each other.

Friends like David, Tim, and Laura have been consistent in their support. David calls me frequently to check in, and Tim has offered to help with simple tasks around the house. Despite her caregiving responsibilities for both her ailing parents, Laura has traveled with me and provided unwavering support. When grief casts its long shadow, friends become the guiding beacons of light that help us navigate through the darkness.

Proverbs 17:17 (NIV) beautifully captures the essence of true friendship: "*A friend loves at all times, and a brother is born for a time of adversity.*" In times of adversity, friends become the family you choose, offering love that transcends the seasons of life. Since my siblings all live in other states, I am grateful for the love and support my friends give.

Friendship shatters the chains of isolation, preventing the despairing echo of "nobody loves me" from taking root. **Ecclesiastes 4:10 (NIV)** emphasizes the strength found in companionship: "*If either of them falls down, one can help the other up. But pity anyone who falls and has no one to help them up.*" In the landscape of grief, friends stand ready to lift us when we stumble.

Welcoming assistance from your friends is an invitation to embrace the shared strength, compassion, and support that true friendship brings. In your vulnerability, you discover the incredible resilience that surfaces when surrounded by a network of caring hearts. As you navigate the path of grief, remember that your friends are not just witnesses to your pain; they are companions on the journey, offering their hands to help you rise and their hearts to share in the ebb and flow of healing.

In this chapter, we've celebrated the incredible impact that friends can have during times of grief. Your friends are not just there to offer a shoulder to lean on; they are there to remind you that you are loved, cherished, and never alone. As you navigate the complexities of grief, let your friends help you bear the burden, find joy in shared moments, and discover hope in their caring gestures.

Remember that you are not a burden to your friends but a beloved friend in need. Lean on them, for they are willing and ready to lift you up when you stumble, bring light into your darkest days, and walk alongside you as you heal and find your way forward. Friends are the treasures that make the journey through grief a little less daunting and a lot more bearable. My challenge to you is to cultivate your friendships with those who are already your friends and try to accept their invitations or find some new friends as you visit grief support groups, go on mission trips, or visit other events.

Chapter 7:

Family Matters

I previously mentioned the large extended family that I have. They have been invaluable in encouraging me, going on vacations with me, and spending time with me. This includes my six siblings and their families, as well as my daughter and son-in-law and my two grandchildren. Sometimes, holding a grandchild is all you need to do to cheer you up in the midst of grief and sadness. My grandchildren, Theo and Autumn, have been sources of joy and fun while keeping me from staying home alone and being sad. My mother-in-law, Joyce, has been living in my basement for years now. We share lots of experiences on a regular basis. Her comment when Carl passed away was that we could take care of each other. Your family also includes your church family, as your local body of Christ is often as close as your blood relatives.

Just four days before our 41st wedding anniversary, my beloved husband Carl departed for his heavenly abode. It was just a week before Thanksgiving, an occasion I had always hosted at our home. The decision to continue this tradition may have seemed daunting, but I was resolute in my choice. My son-in-law, Ben, expressed his concern, telling me, "Pat, you don't have to do this." Meanwhile, my daughter, Michelle, intuitively understood my desire to carry on and remarked, "I think she really wants to." While that first holiday without Carl presented its challenges, I found solace in fulfilling this tradition. Thankfully, my daughter and son-in-law extended their stay, offering a helping hand with the post-feast cleanup.

The outbreak of COVID-19 brought with it the harsh reality of isolation. For six weeks, I was unable to see my beloved grandchildren, unable to share their laughter or offer them a comforting embrace. However, my daughter soon decided it was time for us to reunite, taking the brave step of allowing us to see each other and embrace the risks that came with it.

During this period, I embarked on a road trip with my grandson, Theo, to Texas and back, covering over 2000 miles. My mother-in-law accompanied us, visiting her sister in Texas while I reunited with my sister, Teressa, and brother-in-law, Mike. Though fraught with social distancing measures, this journey was a precious time spent with family during the pandemic. I also had the privilege of taking Theo to Ohio and back, embarking on a journey along Interstate 75. We stopped at various sites along the way, creating lasting memories and bonding with each other. During this time, I realized the significance of family, and the warm embrace of my grandchildren was a balm for my grieving soul. Hugs, in particular, were a cherished rarity that I sorely missed.

As the first New Year's Eve without Carl approached, I decided to spend it at Walt Disney World with my daughter, Michelle, and my grandson, Theo. The diversion provided by the vibrant atmosphere of the theme park was a welcome escape during the holiday season. Holding Theo in my lap as we marveled at the fireworks at Magic Kingdom was far more heartwarming than facing the somber solitude of a New Year's Eve at home.

In an effort to maintain strong bonds with my siblings, we initiated a weekly Zoom meeting with my sisters and sisters-in-law, a tradition that continues to this day. These meetings have evolved into cherished moments of connection and mutual support, even in a post-pandemic world.

My church community played an essential role in providing me with the support I needed during these trying times. Attending virtual Sunday School sessions via Zoom allowed me to see the faces of my fellow churchgoers and strengthened my sense of connection. Over time, my local church congregation formed a tight-knit family, with weekly prayer meetings and heartfelt text messages keeping us united throughout the week.

My second New Year's Eve without Carl proved to be a heartwarming experience spent at the home of Josh and Alaina. Sharing stories and relishing the company of friends brought a much-needed sense of joy. Holidays, with their potential for loneliness, are made all the more meaningful when shared with friends and family.

My own experience as a widow made me acutely aware of the countless others who spend their holidays alone. The stark reality hit me — many people are left without family nearby during the holiday season. This revelation prompted me to take action and seek ways to connect with those who might be experiencing similar feelings of isolation.

I approached Nathan, our senior adult leader, with the idea of hosting a gathering on Christmas Day for those who had nowhere else to be. The event was well-attended, and we decided to continue it the next year. This served as a heartwarming reminder that many people out there need companionship during the holiday season. While some choose to volunteer at charities, serving meals to those in need on holidays, others decide to reach out and extend a helping hand to those who may be feeling the pangs of loneliness. These initiatives help shift the focus from one's own solitude to supporting and uplifting others.

I encourage you to seek out opportunities to spend your holidays in the company of others. If your family is nearby, that's a wonderful option. However, there are countless individuals whose families are miles away, and they, too, yearn for companionship during these times. Embrace invitations or extend your own to invite others into your home.

In the third year after Carl's passing, I hosted a party on New Year's Day for my Sunday school class. It's important not to always wait for others to extend invitations but to take the initiative in inviting friends and acquaintances. Your perspective on life shifts after losing a loved one, making you more aware of those who may be hurting even more deeply.

I have made an effort to plan trips and invite others to go with me. I chose to join a vacation club after Carl passed away. Joining this club made it possible to have travel companions on vacations. Perhaps you have family nearby or even in your house to help encourage and support you. However, if they are not nearby, make plans to go and see them and invite them on trips with you. Invite them to your house for the holidays. Choose to celebrate and enjoy holidays even though they look different. Staying home alone on holidays can lead to depression and loneliness. The time between Christmas Day and New Year's Day is the worst time of the year for depression, so try to plan some social activities to span the holidays. Some of the regular routines of life tend to cause sadness after a loss; however, making new memories by going to new places and doing fun things helps you to see that life goes on and that there's joy in experiencing it with others.

My friends Bill and Piper invited me to join them in Costa Rica for two weeks. Rather than choosing to let myself feel like a third wheel tagging along, I jumped at the chance to be with them on a truly amazing vacation. I invited my sister Natalie and sister-in-law Irene to accompany me on a trip to Hawaii. Is there someone you could bless by inviting them with you on a trip where both of you enjoy experiencing God's great world and His magnificent creation while enjoying each other's company? My challenge to you is to also find meaningful relationships for holidays, as they need to be spent in the company of others.

Chapter 8:

Plan for Your Future and Trust God for It

It can be challenging to think about the future amid grief. When sorrow shrouds your days, it may seem nearly impossible to envision a brighter tomorrow. The pain you experience can sometimes make you feel as if your best days are behind you, and any thought of planning for the future seems distant. But here's the truth: you still have a future, a future that is filled with purpose and promise.

God, the author of your life story, has not abandoned you in your grief. He is still writing your narrative, and He invites you to play a vital role in shaping what's to come. Even through the darkest times, the key to moving forward is to plan for your future and trust God for it.

The Bible reassures you in **Psalm 139:16 (ESV)**: *"Your eyes saw my unformed substance; in your book were written, every one of them, the days that were formed for me, when as yet there was none of them."* This verse reminds you that God is intimately acquainted with every day of your life, from your very beginning to your last breath. He has already written the story of your days, and you can find hope in knowing that He is sovereign over your lifespan.

Now, you might wonder how to plan for a future that feels uncertain and unpredictable. The answer is both simple and profound: Seek God's guidance. He knows the desires of your heart, and He has a purpose for your life. To embrace the future, you must first ask yourself what it is that you truly want and what God may be leading you to do. Your dreams and desires are not insignificant, even in the midst of grief. They are part of the tapestry of your life, and God can use them for His glory.

When Carl passed away, I continued doing mission trips and planned five trips for the first year. I was able to go on only two of those five before COVID-19 shut down the borders of the other countries, and the trips were ultimately canceled. However, since then, life has returned to being more normal, and I am now able to travel and do mission trips again. What this means to you is that even when you make plans, God may allow circumstances that thwart those plans, but times may change again, and you may later be able to fulfill the goals and desires of your heart. Of course, it's also possible that He will send you in a totally different direction, and you may choose to abandon those plans for others that excite you even more.

Proverbs 16:9 (ESV) reminds us, *"The heart of man plans his way, but the Lord establishes his steps."* This verse highlights the partnership between your planning and God's guidance. It's crucial to dream, set goals, and make plans. However, it's equally important to surrender your plans to God and trust that He will establish your steps.

The Bible is filled with verses emphasizing the wisdom of making and pursuing plans. **Proverbs 21:5 (ESV)** encourages us with, *"The plans of the diligent lead surely to abundance, but everyone who is hasty comes only to poverty."* Your diligence and determination to plan for your future, even in the face of grief, can lead to a life of abundance.

I felt that God wanted me to study more Spanish, which has proved useful as I have been on several mission trips to Spanish-speaking countries in South America. In fact, our drive-through prayer ministry recently saw a man drive in who spoke no English. I was able to speak to him in Spanish and share the gospel with him. The Holy Spirit worked in his heart, and he decided to pray to receive Christ as his

Savior. If I had not studied more Spanish and volunteered with this ministry, I would not have had the joy of seeing him come to Jesus.

So, what is it that you want to achieve in your future? Is there a dream or goal that has been tugging at your heart, even in your grief? It may be a career change, a mission trip, further education, writing a book (like I did), or any endeavor that resonates with you. Whatever it is, I encourage you to take that first step. Trust in God's sovereignty over your life and know that your future, though different from what you once envisioned, is still brimming with purpose and potential. Throughout the Bible, we see individuals who made plans and pursued them, trusting in God's guidance and sovereignty. Noah built an ark, David prepared to face Goliath, and Paul embarked on missionary journeys, all following God's call on their lives.

Remember that God's plans for you extend beyond your grief. He is the ultimate author of hope, and your future, though shaped by your past, can be a testament to His grace. Whether you're contemplating a new career, a creative endeavor, or simply seeking joy in your daily life, know that your future is a canvas waiting to be painted with the vibrant colors of God's love and purpose.

Embrace the truth that your days are already written in His book, and as you plan for your future, you can trust Him to guide your steps. Though none of us know how long our journey will be, we can find comfort in knowing that each day is a gift, an opportunity to live out the plans God has in store for us. So take heart and plan for your future, trusting in the sovereign hand that leads you forward.

Here are a few more Bible passages that emphasize the importance of making plans and trusting God in them:

Proverbs 3:5-6 (ESV): *"Trust in the Lord with all your heart, and do not lean on your own understanding. In all your ways acknowledge him, and he will make straight your paths."*

Proverbs 16:3 (ESV): *"Commit your work to the Lord, and your plans will be established."*

James 4:13-15 (ESV): *"Come now, you who say, 'Today or tomorrow we will go into such and such a town and spend a year there and trade and make a profit' — yet you do not know what tomorrow will bring. What is your life? For you are a mist that appears for a little time and then vanishes. Instead, you ought to say, 'If the Lord wills, we will live and do this or that.'"*

Proverbs 19:21 (ESV): *"Many are the plans in the mind of a man, but it is the purpose of the Lord that will stand."*

Psalm 20:4 (ESV): *"May he grant you your heart's desire and fulfill all your plans!"*

Psalm 37:4 (ESV): *"Delight yourself in the Lord, and he will give you the desires of your heart."*

These verses emphasize the importance of seeking God's guidance in your plans, trusting His wisdom and sovereignty, and recognizing that His purposes will ultimately prevail. Planning is an essential part of stewarding the future God has in store for you, even in the midst of grief.

In the pages of 1 Kings 19, we find the prophet Elijah in the throes of despair, isolated in the wilderness. His journey through grief serves as a powerful narrative of resilience, offering inspiration and guidance to those navigating their own paths of sorrow. He ultimately finds a renewed sense of purpose.

Elijah, once victorious on Mount Carmel, found himself fleeing for his life, alone in the wilderness. Elijah's prayer in the wilderness was raw and honest. He poured out his heart to God, expressing his weariness and despair. In his despair, Elijah was exhausted both physically and spiritually. An angel provided him with sustenance, emphasizing the need for self-care during times of grief. Amidst the chaos and storm,

God's voice came to Elijah in a "still, small voice." This gentle whisper signifies the importance of quieting the noise around us and within us. In the process of grief, allowing space for reflection and attentiveness to the "still, small voice" of God can bring comfort and guidance.

Elijah's journey did not end in the wilderness. God gave him a renewed sense of purpose, instructing him to anoint new leaders. This teaches us that, even in our grief, there can be a calling—a new purpose that emerges from the ashes of loss. Exploring opportunities to contribute and serve others can be a transformative step toward healing.

My challenge to you is to let go of the belief that life as you once knew it has ended and, instead, plan for the future God has generously laid out for you. Dare to make plans, set ambitious goals, and schedule exciting trips. Push beyond the boundaries of your former comfort zone and broaden your horizons. Trust in Him as you chart your course forward.

Chapter 9:

It's Okay to Cry and Grieve

Losing my mother, the first immediate family member I had to say goodbye to, was a deeply personal and emotional journey. Despite living in another state for 15 years, our bond remained strong. When she passed away and ascended to heaven, I found myself in a whirlwind of emotions. I had taken time off work in the week leading up to her passing and the week following, a necessary period to grieve, cry, and connect with my family.

The toll of this loss was evident in my physical and emotional well-being. I had even flown back and forth to Oklahoma twice, and the stress began to manifest as chest pains. Concerned about my health, I sought reassurance in a cardiologist's office, where I underwent a comprehensive stress test. At the time, I was around 38 years old, but the weight of my grief was taking a toll on my body. I even had to take some medication to sleep the first few nights after she passed away. Thankfully, this was not as challenging when my father or husband passed.

The truth is that each of us experiences grief in unique ways, and it's crucial to recognize that it's entirely okay to cry and grieve in your own way. It's acceptable to step away from work and seek assistance with daily responsibilities from friends and family. In the initial days after a loss, family and friends often surround us, but as time goes on, the reality of our loved one's absence becomes painfully clear. We long for their presence, the conversations we shared, and the moments we cherished together.

Certain times of the day become poignant reminders of our loss because we associate those moments with the presence of the one we've lost. It's a challenging time, and while well-meaning friends and family may encourage us to keep busy, there are days when all we want to do is stare off into space, lost in our thoughts.

There's a significant disconnect between well-intentioned advice and the reality of grief. Staying busy doesn't erase the pain; it merely masks it temporarily. If possible, consider taking additional time off from work to allow yourself more room to heal from the emotional strain of the funeral and the initial waves of grief. I understand this isn't always feasible.

The Bible provides comforting verses that remind you that God is present in your suffering. **In Exodus 3:7 (NIV)**, it is written, "*The Lord said, 'I have indeed seen the misery of my people in Egypt. I have heard them crying out because of their slave drivers, and I am concerned about their suffering.'*" This verse serves as a testament to God's compassion for His people in times of distress.

The words of David in **Psalm 56:8-9 (NIV)** further emphasize this divine care: "*You keep track of all my sorrows. You have collected all my tears in your bottle. You have recorded each one in your book. My enemies will turn back when I call for help. By this, I will know that God is for me.*" These verses were written during a challenging period in David's life while the Philistines held him captive. They serve as a reminder that God diligently keeps track of our sorrows, ensuring no tear escapes His notice. The knowledge that God is with us, even in our tears, provides an incredible sense of comfort.

In the book of John, we find the shortest verse in the Bible, **John 11:35**, which simply states, "*Jesus wept.*" Even though Jesus knew He would raise Lazarus from the dead, He wept at the tomb. Why, then, was He weeping? Was He manifesting His human emotion of sadness at losing a friend? Was He sad that death existed at all? Since death didn't exist before the fall of man, He may have been grieving the lost state of mankind. The first loss that ever occurred was the loss of an intimate relationship between God and Adam and Eve in the Garden of Eden. Since that time, we have all faced losses. Loss is inevitable. The last time I checked, the probability of dying (if Jesus doesn't return first) was 100%. We all face death, and we lose those close to us.

My mother-in-law, Joyce, received valuable advice from her doctor after losing her husband to heaven: a good cry is often the best medicine. Loss brings genuine suffering and real tears. It wasn't the original design when God created the world. His perfect design was free from death, suffering, and pain. Yet, we now face losses and the inevitable reality of death.

Remember that it's vital to give yourself the space and time to grieve and cry. Allow your emotions to flow naturally. Consider taking time off work, and don't be afraid to seek help when you need it. Above all, hold onto the knowledge that one day, as promised in **Revelation 21:4 (NIV)**, "*He will wipe every tear from their eyes. There will be no* *more death or mourning or crying or pain, for the old order of things has passed away."*

My challenge to you is to embrace your grief. Allow the tears to flow when they need to. Take time off if possible, and provide yourself with the time and space to process your emotions. Always keep in mind the comforting promise of the ultimate future when Jesus returns, ensuring there will be no more pain, sorrow, or tears. In that reassurance, find comfort and gratitude for a brighter tomorrow.

Chapter 10:

Do What You Need to Do

Life can feel as if it has been turned upside down in the aftermath of a significant loss. The burden of grief often makes even the simplest tasks appear impossible, leaving you feeling overwhelmed and uncertain about how to proceed. In such moments, it is essential to remind yourself that taking practical steps to care for your well-being is a crucial part of the healing journey.

After Carl's passing, I chose to make several changes to promote my well-being. I updated my will, embarked on a weight loss journey, committed to daily walks around the neighborhood for approximately 30 minutes each day, and joined a gym that offered classes focusing on strength training. The months I spent caring for Carl had left me neglecting my self-care and the demands of his illness made it impossible for me to find time to go to a gym. When grief strikes, it is common to overlook practical matters, but addressing these issues is a vital aspect of the healing process.

Here are some steps you should consider taking to update your legal and financial matters: Review your will, estate plans, and beneficiary designations. If necessary, consult an attorney or financial planner to ensure your wishes are in order. This preparation can provide peace of mind and clarity during uncertain times.

Your choice of food plays a significant role in your physical and emotional well-being. During times of grief, there is a temptation to turn to comfort foods, but nourishing your body with healthy meals can boost your mood and energy levels. Proper nutrition is essential for maintaining your strength during this challenging period. In the years leading up to Carl's death, I had allowed my weight to increase. However, despite the difficulties, I intentionally embarked on a healthy eating program and shed a considerable amount of weight during the pandemic. Many people were not dining out due to the pandemic, providing the perfect opportunity for me to take control of my eating habits at home.

Regular physical activity has been scientifically proven to elevate mood and reduce stress. Even a short daily walk can significantly impact your overall well-being. Do not underestimate the power of movement to help you through your grief. Going to the gym strengthens your muscles and exposes you to social interaction, preventing you from isolating yourself at home. The American Heart Association recommends at least 150 minutes of moderate-intensity aerobic exercise per week, 75 minutes of vigorous aerobic activity, or a combination of both, preferably spread throughout the week. However, only about one in five adults and teenagers get enough exercise to maintain good health.

When I take my neighborhood walks, I often listen to the Bible or engage in a podcast or Bible study by preachers such as Rick Warren, J. D. Greear, or Louie Giglio. Pairing physical activity with something enjoyable, like a podcast or music, makes it seem less daunting. In fact, I find that walking has become a time of worship for me. A good walking buddy can also be a great motivator to help you stay accountable.

Researchers have analyzed sitting time and activity levels in numerous studies and have found that those who sit for more than eight hours a day with no physical activity face a risk similar to that posed by obesity and smoking. This phenomenon has even earned a name - sitting disease. Hence, it is essential to break up prolonged periods of sitting by engaging in light activity regularly. Even my Fitbit helps me ensure I get 250 steps every hour, reminding me ten minutes before the hour to complete those steps between 9 a.m. and 6 p.m.

Muscle-strengthening activities, such as resistance or weight training, should be conducted at least two days a week. Aging often results in a loss of muscle mass, especially in the upper leg muscles. This loss can make it challenging for older individuals to transition from a sitting to a standing position without assistance. Deconditioning of muscles can exacerbate this issue, particularly after an injury or surgery. To address this, I have chosen to participate in a gym class that lasts for one hour twice a week. Exercising with others not only strengthens muscles but also serves as a motivating factor to keep up with the class.

Grief is a journey that demands attention to both practical and emotional needs. Seeking assistance or proactively caring for yourself is not a sign of weakness; rather, it reflects courage and resilience.

It's important to remember that healing is not a linear process. Some days will be more challenging than others. Nevertheless, by addressing practical matters and nurturing your spiritual and emotional well-being, you are taking the necessary steps toward growth and eventual restoration.

Amid your pain, my challenge to you is to prioritize self-care. Seek professional guidance when needed, pay attention to your physical health, and never underestimate the power of spiritual and emotional well-being. While you endure your pain, you are also sowing the seeds of resilience, strength, and hope that will guide you towards a brighter future.

Chapter 11:

Don't Isolate

The U.S. Surgeon General, Dr. Vivek Murthy, has issued an advisory recognizing loneliness as a growing public health crisis in the United States. His warning emphasizes that our society faces an epidemic of loneliness and isolation that has not been given the attention it deserves. This issue, prevalent both individually and collectively, negatively impacts our physical and emotional well-being and the fiber of our communities.

Social connections, vital to our health and well-being, have been diminishing, especially among young people, and the alarming statistic indicates that approximately half of all adults experience loneliness. The consequences of this loneliness extend to the economic realm, translating into billions of dollars in healthcare costs. The health risks are severe, encompassing heart disease, stroke, and dementia. The solution is clear: we must rebuild these connections to combat this growing crisis, prioritizing it as we have with other pressing public health issues such as tobacco use, obesity, and substance abuse. By doing so, we can foster a healthier, more resilient, and less lonely nation.

In light of these findings, it is evident that the digital connections created through social media platforms do not suffice. These connections often remain superficial, unable to meet the need for deeper, more meaningful relationships rooted in genuine sharing of thoughts and emotions. Real, in-depth connections, enriched by transparency, are the remedy for loneliness, and studies have shown that such connections can reduce the risk of early death by up to 50%.

Many individuals struggle with loneliness yet hesitate to acknowledge it, leading to a self-perpetuating cycle. As a feeling, loneliness is often accompanied by physical symptoms, driving those affected further away from potential sources of support. By refusing to admit your loneliness, you only isolate yourself more, unable to recognize that you are not alone in experiencing these emotions.

It is crucial to differentiate between solitude, the physical state of being alone, and loneliness, which pertains to feeling disconnected from others. To combat loneliness, it is necessary to actively interact with people throughout the day. While it is possible to be with only one person and not feel lonely because of deep connections to that one person and to yourself, many individuals find themselves surrounded by others but remain lonely because they are unwilling to open up and share their thoughts and feelings. To overcome loneliness, you must move beyond this barrier.

Breaking free from the cycle of loneliness involves a choice – the choice to be vulnerable with others. It means sharing deep emotions, hurts, or needs, signifying a willingness to reveal yourself as a real person with genuine emotions and requirements. This is not a call to complain or seek attention but rather an invitation to demonstrate that you are a human with authentic feelings and needs. The path to recovery also requires being physically present with others, as spending the entire day on social media does not alleviate loneliness – it exacerbates it. This digital engagement not only intensifies the sense of disconnection but also amplifies feelings of isolation. It exposes individuals to the apparent joys of others, thereby underscoring their own aloneness.

God designed you for relationships, as even in the Book of Genesis, when He created Adam, He recognized that it was not good for man to be alone. This fundamental need for human connection endures as you navigate life's challenges, for you are never truly alone. In times of grief or distress, God provides comfort through the people He has placed in your life. As you navigate these difficult experiences, it is vital to share your burdens with those who care for you, alleviating the weight on your shoulders.

After Carl's passing, I attended GriefShare, a program that employs small groups, videos, and workbooks to facilitate the healing process after the loss of a loved one. This platform offers a safe space for individuals to open up and share their experiences and emotions with others who are also grieving. Attending these sessions and choosing to be vulnerable with others played a pivotal role in my healing journey, and I wholeheartedly recommend it as a valuable resource.

While text messages, emails, and social media platforms can provide a degree of connection, the depth of these connections is what truly matters. The focus should not be on the quantity but on the quality of these relationships. Attending a large congregation on Sundays can lead to further isolation if you merely walk in and out without engaging in meaningful interactions. It is imperative that you embrace true connections by engaging with others on a deeper level, where genuine thoughts and feelings are shared. Responding to a simple question like, "How are you?" with a candid answer can be the first step in forging genuine connections. By choosing to be vulnerable and transparent, you can begin to break free from the chains of loneliness.

God has ordained that we, His people, serve as the hands and feet of Jesus, offering support, companionship, and love to one another. He has designed you to thrive in relationships, as every burden becomes lighter when shared. The loss of a close relationship underscores the need to fill that void with new, healthy connections. These connections should not be confused with intimate relationships or rushed into. They are formed out of the genuine love and support that can be provided by friends and family who are willing to listen, care, and share. We receive the guidance and comfort necessary to heal and move forward by leaning on one another.

My family and friends often tease me about talking a lot or sharing a lot. I feel that this is a necessary behavior to help others know you on a deeper level. If you aren't willing to share, how can anyone really know you? Hiding deeper feelings and needs is a contributor to loneliness. You have to be willing to open up and be transparent with some friends or family members to really connect on a level that matters. Superficial connections should be reserved for acquaintances and not friends.

I challenge you, as you struggle with the profound issue of loneliness, to recognize its gravity and take steps to be vulnerable with those who are willing to love and support you. Seek out genuine connections, as loneliness is a significant problem that demands acknowledgment and action.

Chapter 12:

Have Fun

I know some people who don't seem to know how to have fun. During times of grief, it's important to learn how to have fun again. On the anniversary of the day I met Carl, which occurred almost a year after he went to heaven, I woke up feeling cold and low on energy. My grandson Theo was at my house as he had spent the night with me. For some reason, he was in one of those moods where he didn't want to do anything with me. Instead, he wanted to play alone in his room. I knew that if we played a game together, it would lift my spirits. So I told him to get in the car because I would take him somewhere fun. I took him for the first time to Urban Air, an indoor play area featuring trampolines, ziplines, sky hikes, a climbing wall, go-karts, and an indoor skydiving area. He loved it, but more than that, I loved it. Over time, we explored all of it, including indoor skydiving and virtual reality games.

Whenever you feel blue, moving your body tends to help. Throughout the years, you need to plan some fun in your life. My friend Lewann gave us a snow cone machine, and we love to make snow cones with sugar-free syrup and just enjoy them together. Playing ball or swimming in the summer are fun activities for me to do with Theo and Autumn. We love feeding animals and seeing them at Yellow River Wildlife Sanctuary or Zoo Atlanta. We got season passes to Walt Disney World for one year and Dollywood for another. I am not a bystander in any of these activities because I believe you should have fun. God gave you a life to live - not to sit and feel sorry for yourself.

This year, Autumn and I got season passes to Stone Mountain and loved to go to all the festivals there. She told her mama that she loves to go up to the top of the mountain because it's awesome. I love to stand on the mountain and view God's creation, especially in the fall when all the trees are beautifully colored.

When Carl left for heaven, he had some Dave and Buster's tickets left in his billfold. Theo and I spent time together and played games there. Autumn and I like to go to Chuck E Cheese and play games. Michelle and I went to a Paint Your Own painting class, and I also went with my friend

Beth. These are activities that are creative, but they are fun, especially if you've never tried your hand at it.

Michelle, Theo, Autumn, and I have been to pick our own apples, corn mazes, and pumpkin farms, and we have driven through animal safaris and butterfly sanctuaries. We've been to fairs, farmers' markets, and fall festivals. Having fun is not masking grief. It's working through grief by enjoying the events and the joy of experiencing new things with people you love. The smiles and laughter of the grandchildren and shared experiences and memories made together are truly fun.

In **Ecclesiastes 3:4 (NIV),** The Bible talks about having a time for everything and specifically says: *"a time to weep and a time to laugh, a time to mourn and a time to dance."* Most of life is more fun when shared with someone else. If the one who shared all your secrets, hobbies, and shared memories is no longer here, you must find new hobbies and make new shared memories with others.

The Bible speaks quite a lot about happiness, laughter, and joy. Let's look at some of the Scriptures that have to do with joy and laughter:

Proverbs 14:13 (NIV): *"Even in laughter the heart may ache, and rejoicing may end in grief."*

Jeremiah 31:13 (NIV): *"Then young women will dance and be glad, young men and old as well. I will turn their mourning into gladness; I will give them comfort and joy instead of sorrow."*

Proverbs 17:22 (NIV): *"A cheerful heart is good medicine, but a crushed spirit dries up the bones."*

Psalm 126:2-3 (NIV): *"Our mouths were filled with laughter, our tongues with songs of joy. Then it was said among the nations, 'The Lord has done great things for them.' The Lord has done great things for us, and we are filled with joy."*

Psalm 30:11 (NIV): *"You turned my wailing into dancing; you removed my sackcloth and clothed me with joy."*

Proverbs 15:13 (NIV): *"A happy heart makes the face cheerful, but heartache crushes the spirit."*

Psalm 118:24 (NIV): *"The Lord has done it this very day; let us rejoice today and be glad."*

Ecclesiastes 8:15 (NIV): *"So I commend the enjoyment of life because there is nothing better for a person under the sun than to eat and drink and be glad. Then joy will accompany them in their toil all the days of the life God has given them under the sun."*

Job 8:21 (NIV): *"He will yet fill your mouth with laughter and your lips with shouts of joy."*

John 16:22, 24 (NIV): *"So with you: Now is your time of grief, but I will see you again and you will rejoice, and no one will take away your joy. ... Until now you have not asked for anything in my name. Ask and you will receive, and your joy will be complete."*

Hebrews 12:2 (NIV): *"fixing our eyes on Jesus, the pioneer and perfecter of faith. For the joy set before him he endured the cross, scorning its shame, and sat down at the right hand of the throne of God."*

Nehemiah 8:10 (NIV): *"Nehemiah said, 'Go and enjoy choice food and sweet drinks, and send some to those who have nothing prepared. This day is holy to our Lord. Do not grieve, for the joy of the Lord is your strength.'"*

Isaiah 35:10 (NIV): *"and those the Lord has rescued will return. They will enter Zion with singing; everlasting joy will crown their heads. Gladness and joy will overtake them, and sorrow and sighing will flee away."*

Galatians 5:22 (NIV): *"But the fruit of the Spirit is love, joy, peace, forbearance, kindness, goodness, faithfulness."*

Happiness can coexist with sorrow, but joy can endure as a fruit of the spirit. Joyful living is a soul-satisfying pleasure, often found in simple daily pleasures. Children and grandchildren are sources of joy, their laughter filling our hearts with gratitude. Staying active is essential for mental well-being. Life is more enjoyable when shared, and if a loved one is no longer present, find new hobbies and make new memories with others.

Psalm 127:3 (NIV): *"Children are a heritage from the Lord, offspring a reward from him."*

Proverbs 17:6 (NIV): *"Children's children are a crown to the aged, and parents are the pride of their children."*

So what do you like to do for fun? There are so many fun activities, and you are not meant to stay home and be alone. Fun can be found with simple things like feeding some corn to the ducks on the lake behind my house.

My challenge to you is to explore the opportunities for fun around you, create plans, and enjoy the simple pleasures of life. Whether with a friend, grandchild, or child, rediscover the laughter of innocence and embrace the joy God intended for His people.

Chapter 13:

Get Right With God

The death of King Uzziah holds great significance in the book of Isaiah as it marks a pivotal moment in the prophet's life and in the religious history of ancient Israel. When Uzziah died, Isaiah had a vision of the Lord, a profound and transformative experience. Isaiah and the Israelites may not have seen God clearly when King Uzziah was alive. When he died, Isaiah had good reason to be discouraged and disillusioned because a great king had passed away, and his life ended tragically due to his pride. (see Second Kings 15 and Second Chronicles 26 also)

Isaiah 6:1 (NIV) says: *"In the year that King Uzziah died, I saw the Lord, high and exalted, seated on a throne; and the train of his robe filled the temple."* This encounter symbolized the transition from an earthly king to a higher divine authority, underscoring the sovereignty of God over human rulers. Isaiah's vision of the Lord emphasized God's majesty and holiness, highlighting the need for reverence and obedience to His will. It served as a call to faithfulness and a reminder of God's enduring presence amid political changes.

Reflecting on the passing of my husband, Carl, who played a significant role in my life for 41 years, I couldn't help but compare it to Isaiah's experience. Sometimes, it takes a tragedy to reveal what truly matters. Just as Isaiah may not have fully seen God's glory during King Uzziah's reign, I had, at times, elevated Carl to a place in my heart reserved for God alone. It's a struggle I'm not proud of, and Carl rightly encouraged me to repent. His passing, while heartbreaking, ultimately unified my heart's focus. It was a powerful moment when I said, "Lord, it's just You and me again."

Recalling my childhood, I cherished a deep love for Jesus, whom I knew was the greatest presence in my life. But as I fell in love with Carl, my heart became divided. The profound relationship I once had with Christ got overshadowed, and it's a time of my life that I now feel ashamed of. Just as I had to repent for my misplaced priorities, maybe there's something in your life that requires repentance — a sense of pride, entitlement, or even disappointment with God for not answering your prayers as you hoped. God's forgiveness is always available. **1 John 1:9 (NIV)** assures us: *"If we confess our sins, he is faithful and just and will forgive us our sins and purify us from all unrighteousness."*

God often reveals our wrong motives, thoughts, attitudes, or actions. It's our duty to recognize these sins, repent, and ask for His forgiveness. Before my mission trip to Indonesia during the COVID-19 pandemic, my preparation included the possibility of needing Paxlovid in case I fell ill with the virus. My doctor prescribed it and sent the prescription to the pharmacy. However, things took an unexpected turn when the pharmacist contacted me before filling the prescription. Asked whether I had tested positive for COVID-19, I initially replied, "No, I just need it for my mission trip in case I get sick while there."

When the pharmacist hesitated and explained that they couldn't dispense the medication without a positive test result, I relayed the situation to my doctor, who attempted to send the prescription to another pharmacy. Unfortunately, the second pharmacist followed up with the same question: "Did you test positive for COVID-19?" This time, I quietly replied, "No," and when he asked me to clarify, I hesitantly said, "Yes." In that moment, the conviction of God's Holy Spirit washed over me, reminding me of the truth I had strayed from. I obtained the medication I wanted. However, as I was driving home, God told me, "You told him you had a positive test, so you are going to have one." Little did I know that my dishonesty would have that consequence. During our mission trip to Indonesia, five members of our team, including myself, tested positive for COVID-19. I was quarantined in a hotel in Jakarta, providing me with ample time for reflection, repentance, and conversations with God.

My heart was heavy with regret as I realized that I might not have contracted COVID-19 if I had trusted God's plan instead of resorting to deceit. When I shared this story with friends, some attempted to downplay my lie as a "little white lie" justified by the need for medication. My response was, "No, I didn't have to lie. I should have trusted God." I emphasized that no lie is truly insignificant and that trusting God, even in challenging circumstances, should always be our first choice. This painful lesson emphasized the gravity of all sins, regardless of their perceived magnitude.

Job repented in **Job 42:1-6 (NIV)**: *"Then Job replied to the Lord: 'I know that you can do all things; no purpose of yours can be thwarted.' You asked, "Who is this that obscures my plans without knowledge?" Surely I spoke of things I did not understand, things too wonderful for me to know. You said, "Listen now, and*

I will speak; I will question you, and you shall answer me." My ears had heard of you but now my eyes have seen you. Therefore I despise myself and repent in dust and ashes.'" Job repented and confessed, recognizing God's infinite wisdom and his own limited understanding. King David repented of his sins of adultery, murder, and arrogance. David's heartfelt repentance in Psalm 51 revealed the transformation that occurs when we turn from our sins and seek God's mercy. The repentance of Job and David serve as powerful examples of acknowledging our sins and seeking God's forgiveness. Their stories emphasize the profound impact of repentance on our relationship with God.

My challenge to you is to shift your focus from the sadness that causes grief to the weight of your own sin before a holy God. Deal with it honestly and repent. Any sin creates a separation between you and God. Seek reconciliation and a right relationship with Him, for He is merciful and just.

Chapter 14:
Find Your Purpose

I recall a story shared by Josh McDowell from some time ago. It was about a headhunter who had a unique approach to interviews. To set the stage, he would casually offer his interviewee a drink, loosen his own tie, and put his feet on the desk. The goal was to create a relaxed atmosphere before springing the big question, "What's your purpose in life?" One particular day, he followed his usual routine: offered the drink and started to loosen his tie, but the interviewee politely declined the beverage. With a sense of curiosity, the headhunter propped his feet up, hoping to catch the man off guard. When he finally posed the question, the man replied without hesitation, "To go to heaven and take as many people with me as I possibly can." This story always serves as a poignant reminder that we all have a purpose in life, even when it might appear obscured by the clouds of grief.

My daddy used to say, "Everyone needs something to do, someone to love, and something to look forward to." Let's delve deeper into what he meant. A void emerges in our lives after a loss, be it a family member, job, friend, or ability to perform certain tasks due to declining health. Our minds grieve this loss, and we naturally seek to fill that void. The critical decision, however, lies in what we choose to fill it with. The world offers numerous options, but it's essential to remember that our time is a precious asset. Making unwise choices can lead to long-term unhappiness or defeat. For instance, rushing into a new relationship, particularly an intimate one, may bring temporary happiness, but it can result in prolonged pain or even agony.

Matthew 6:33 (NIV) urges us, "*But seek first his kingdom and his righteousness, and all these things will be given to you as well.*" This verse emphasizes the importance of seeking God and His righteousness as a priority. Seeking God means turning to Him for comfort, strength, and reassurance while acknowledging His attributes and capabilities. God has a unique plan for each of us. When we genuinely seek God first, we remain focused on His purpose for us and trust Him to care for us. Instead of panicking or withdrawing, we surrender all our worries and anxieties to Him.

Matthew 22:37-39 (NIV) states: *"Jesus replied: 'Love the Lord your God with all your heart and with all your soul and with all your mind.' This is the first and greatest commandment. And the second is like it: 'Love your neighbor as yourself.'"* We should direct our love primarily toward Jesus. In turn, this love should extend to others.

John 10:10 (NIV) affirms, *"The thief comes only to steal and kill and destroy; I have come that they may have life, and have it to the full."* Unlike a thief who takes, Jesus is a giver. An abundant life refers to a life filled with joy and strength. It signifies eternal life. In John 17:3 (NIV), we find that eternal life is defined by knowing the one true God and Jesus Christ personally, not just in theory. It's not solely about acknowledging His existence but rather having invited Him to be your Savior, with His Holy Spirit residing within you.

The essence of this message relates directly to the concept of having something to do, someone to love, and something to look forward to. Recognizing Jesus as your Savior provides the love you need, preventing you from filling the void with the wrong relationships. Moreover, He guides you through His Holy Spirit, offering clear direction. Having something to do entails engaging in meaningful activities rather than mindlessly going about daily chores, which can lead to emptiness and sadness. God intended life to be abundantly fulfilling. What excites you? What does God prompt you to do in the years ahead? It's crucial to seek His guidance through prayer, recognizing that prayer is a direct line to Him. Many people limit their prayers to thanking God for daily provisions and seeking comfort when they cry out for help. Yet, genuine prayer may sometimes be agonizing as it involves raw emotions and battles against the darkness in one's life. Prayer is a powerful tool that moves the forces of darkness, allowing God to work on your behalf. **Daniel 10:10-14 (NIV)** illustrates the concept of spiritual warfare within prayer:

10 A hand touched me and set me trembling on my hands and knees. 11 He said, "Daniel, you who are highly esteemed, consider carefully the words I am about to speak to you, and stand up, for I have now been sent to you." And when he said this to me, I stood up trembling.

12 Then he continued, "Do not be afraid, Daniel. Since the first day that you set your mind to gain understanding and to humble yourself before your God, your words were heard, and I have come in response to them. 13 But the prince of the Persian kingdom resisted me twenty-one days. Then Michael, one of the chief princes, came to help me, because I was detained there with the king of Persia. 14 Now I have come to explain to you what will happen to your people in the future, for the vision concerns a time yet to come."

While you may not encounter an angel in response to your prayers, you will receive answers. Sometimes, the answers come through Scripture; at other times, they manifest as nudges from the Holy Spirit. Recognizing God's direction is essential, as it may diverge from your usual thoughts and actions. Capturing this guidance and following it is vital. For example, after Carl passed away, I felt led to study Spanish, even though it wasn't in my plans. Although I didn't know it then, this decision prepared me for mission trips to South America and drive-through prayer encounters, such as with Edson, whom I introduced to Jesus in Spanish.

Our Father in Heaven knows our past, present, and future, directing us toward tasks that will have meaning. We are not meant to pass our days in quiet despair, just puttering around the house and engaging in meaningless activities.

Scripture also warns against idleness:

Proverbs 16:27-29 from The Living Bible (TLB): "*27 Idle hands are the devil's workshop; idle lips are his mouthpiece. 28 An* *evil man sows strife; gossip separates the best of friends. 29 Wickedness loves company – and leads others into sin."*

2 Thessalonians 3:11 (NIV) notes: *"For we hear that some among you are idle and disruptive. They are not busy; they are busybodies."*

1 Timothy 5:13 (NIV) adds: *"Besides, they get into the habit of being idle and going about from house to house. And not only do they become idlers, but also busybodies who talk nonsense, saying things they ought not to."*

Songwriters Luke Smallbone, Joel David Smallbone, Sean Maxwell Douglas, Joshua Kerr, and Jimmie Allen wrote a song called "What Are We Waiting For?" It was made popular by For King & Country with a phrase that really applies to those who are grieving as well as everyone else:

"So what are we waiting for? What are we waiting for? Why are we wasting all the time like someone's making more? What are we praying for? What are we saving for? What if we could be the light that no one could ignore? What are we waiting for?" This song conveys the urgency of not squandering time, emphasizing that we can't act as though there's an endless supply of it. Time is a valuable commodity meant for investing in God's kingdom work, often by impacting the lives of others. What is your calling? What should you pray about to gain guidance and move forward through grief?

The third component of my dad's statement is something to look forward to. As Christians, we anticipate heaven and reuniting with our loved ones who have gone before us. Our ultimate joy is seeing Jesus. However, in the present, life continues for those who remain. Focusing on the heavenly realm should not disconnect us from those around us who are currently suffering. Make the most of your time. For instance, I know a seminary professor who, during chemotherapy for cancer, offered hope and led people to accept Jesus as their Savior. His joy in the midst of pain served as a testament to God's power, illustrating that even in challenging circumstances, we can be a beacon of hope for others. Rather than waking up each day and retreating under the covers in self-pity, pray for opportunities to use your grief to aid others. There are numerous people in the world who are hurting, and you have a message to share. If you are willing, God will use you, and you can look forward to helping others discover the hope, peace, joy, and love that He offers.

What are you looking forward to? I eagerly anticipate speaking to groups, coaching individuals, embarking on adventures to share Jesus' message, engaging in drive-through prayer, and working with individuals to assist those facing hardships. The prospect of mission trips and exploring God's creation excites me, filling me with indescribable joy as I obey Him. If you feel a lack of joy or peace after a loss, ask Him to grant it to you. These are the fruit of the Holy Spirit in your life, and you can request more of them.

God loves you and delights in bestowing good gifts upon His children. **James 1:17 (NIV)** reminds us: *"Every good and perfect gift is from above, coming down from the Father of the heavenly lights, who does not change like shifting shadows."* He is the source of unwavering light, unlike shifting shadows. Turning away from Him leads deeper into darkness.

When Carl and I searched for a new house back in 2005, I offered a heartfelt prayer before setting out with the real estate agent. I asked God to reveal something truly extraordinary, a special gift from Him, during our evening of house-hunting. It was at the very last house we visited that God granted my prayer. As I gazed out the back of the house, I was greeted by a breathtaking view of a beautiful lake. That picturesque view became my special gift from

God. We ended up purchasing that house, and to this day, I continue to relish the beauty of that lake. It's a reminder that God delights in surprising us with wonderful gifts because He loves us so dearly. The question is: wouldn't you want to reciprocate that love?

This chapter highlights the importance of having someone to love, something meaningful to do, and something to look forward to. It shows that you still have a purpose in your life. One of my cherished Bible verses is **Proverbs 3:5-6 (NIV)**: *"Trust in the Lord with all your heart and lean not on your understanding; in all your ways submit to Him, and He will make your paths straight."* This verse reminds you that He is your Someone to love, His will is your something to do, and if you trust Him, He provides direction to guide you so you have something to look forward to in the present world as well as seeing Him in heaven in the future.

My challenge to you is to love God with all your heart, discern His purpose for you, and eagerly anticipate each day as He provides opportunities to share His love with others. You are here for a reason, and that purpose is to love Him and bring His light to those who need Him.

Chapter 15:

Listen to God's Voice

When I was 25 years old, Carl was pursuing a Master of Divinity degree at Southwestern Baptist Theological Seminary in Fort Worth, Texas. During a spring break in March, he journeyed to Montana to lead special services at a local church while I remained home, working as a dietitian at Huguley Memorial Medical Center. The time I had alone away from work became an opportunity for me to draw closer to the Lord.

At that point in my life, I had been diligently reading through the Bible, and I had reached the book of Numbers. Simultaneously, I was immersed in the sounds of my 8-track tapes featuring the uplifting harmonies of the Imperials. One particular song stood out, with lyrics that seemed to leap off the tape: "I know you can do it this time if you'll just try again."

This period of reflection and prayer was a pivotal moment as I sought further direction for my life. Then, I came across Numbers 8:24 in the Bible, which stated that the Levites began their temple service training at the age of 25. I felt God's message was clear: "Pat, you're 25 now. It's time to embark on the training for the purpose I have called you for. I know you can do it this time."

With this sense of divine calling, I asked God for confirmation through Carl. Upon his return, we took a walk around the seminary mobile home park where we resided, and I shared the Bible verse, the song, and my interpretation with him. Carl, ever supportive, wholeheartedly believed that if God was leading me toward medical school, I should pursue it, and he pledged his unwavering support. I had never previously applied, and some coursework was necessary to meet the requirements for medical school, so I enrolled in the required courses at the University of Texas at Arlington, setting my journey towards medical school in motion at the age of 25.

I applied to ten medical schools and was fortunate enough to secure interviews with six of them. During the interviews at the initial three or four schools, the interviewers expressed that I was precisely the type of candidate they were seeking and that acceptance was highly likely. Yet, these schools were scattered across Texas, from Galveston to Houston and Lubbock, making it difficult to choose one if offered admission by all of them. Consequently, Carl and I decided to pray for divine guidance. We prayed that God would open the door to the medical school He intended for me and firmly shut the doors to all others.

My fifth interview was at the University of North Texas Health Science Center/Texas College of Osteopathic Medicine in Fort Worth, where I met Dr. Clyde Gallehugh, one of the interviewers. Dr. Gallehugh believed that a calling to medicine was similar to Carl's calling to ministry, and he asked me to share my own "call experience." I recounted the Numbers 8:24 Bible verse, the Imperials' song, and how I had confirmed this with Carl. Dr. Gallehugh, who happened to be a deacon in a Baptist church and a Sunday school teacher, probed further, asking how I planned to teach the upcoming Sunday's lesson. Unbeknownst to me, he was examining whether we had the same lesson and wished to hear my perspective on it. The interview was, to say the least, an intriguing one.

The very next day, while working as a dietitian at Raleigh Hills Hospital in Dallas, I received a phone call that was nothing short of a shock. I was informed that I had been accepted into the medical school in Fort Worth. In light of this acceptance, I promptly canceled my sixth school interview. Strangely, the other four schools neither accepted me nor issued any form of denial. It became evident that God had chosen to open one door while closing all the others. I had only been accepted at the Fort Worth institution, where Carl could continue his work at Southwestern Baptist Theological Seminary as the placement director in the Church-Minister Relations office. Remarkably, this alignment allowed us to reside in a familiar city, where I could pursue my medical studies, and Carl could complete a second Master's degree. Dr. Gallehugh played a significant role in facilitating Christian students' entry into the school, ultimately placing me in an environment where I could thrive in both my medical training and personal life.

Do you listen to God's voice and pray specifically for what God wants you to do next? He is usually loud and clear. If you need help, contact me, as I can help you get to where you can discern His voice. It isn't always a still, small voice like Elijah's encounter was. Many times, God speaks very clearly. I'm amazed at the times in the Bible when kings, disciples, apostles, and prophets knew exactly what God told them to do. These passages illustrate this truth:

Joshua 7:10-15 - After Israel's defeat at Ai, Joshua inquired of the Lord to understand the reason for their failure. God revealed Achan's sin, which led to their defeat.

1 Samuel 23:9-12 - David inquired of the Lord about Saul's intentions, and God instructed him to leave Keilah to avoid Saul's attack.

2 Samuel 2:1-4 - After the death of Saul and his sons, David inquired of the Lord about going to Hebron, where God confirmed his decision to go.

1 Kings 3:5-14 - Solomon, the son of David, inquired of God for wisdom to rule God's people. God granted his request and gave him wisdom and more.

2 Chronicles 20:3-17 - Jehoshaphat, king of Judah, inquired of the Lord when facing a great enemy army. God gave them a clear strategy and delivered them from their enemies.

1 Kings 18:21-39 - The prophet Elijah inquired of God before his confrontation with the prophets of Baal. God answered by sending fire from heaven to consume his offering, affirming His presence and power.

Judges 6:36-40 - Gideon placed a fleece of wool on the ground and asked God to make it wet with dew while keeping the ground dry and then vice versa. God answered both requests, demonstrating His guidance to Gideon.

1 Samuel 3:1-18 - The boy Samuel, while living with Eli, the priest, heard the voice of God calling him multiple times. After seeking guidance from Eli, Samuel received a direct message from God, which set him on the path of prophecy.

Ezra 8:21-23 - Before embarking on a journey, Ezra proclaimed a fast to seek God's guidance and protection for his group. God answered their prayers by granting them safe passage and protecting their possessions.

Acts 9:1-19 - Saul (later known as Paul) had a dramatic encounter with Jesus on the road to Damascus. He heard the voice of the Lord and received direct instructions on how to proceed.

Isaiah 38:1-5 - In response to Hezekiah's prayer and sincere devotion, God granted him an additional fifteen years of life.

It's clear from these passages that God gives specific directions and guidance when you ask. He is still doing it today. My challenge to you is to ask God specific questions and listen to His voice. He will show you what to do next. Many people, after loss, have trouble focusing and making decisions. God's answers will provide clear direction.

Chapter 16:

Be Filled With the Holy Spirit

During my teenage years in Broken Arrow, Oklahoma, attending Falls Creek was one of the main activities for Baptist youth or anyone with Baptist friends. Falls Creek is the world's largest Baptist camp, welcoming thousands of teenagers each summer to stay in cabins with their church groups or as guests of those groups. Since I belonged to a very small church, we teamed up with Eleventh Street Baptist Church in Tulsa to make the annual pilgrimage to Falls Creek from the time I finished sixth grade through high school.

When I was fourteen years old, we had a summer youth minister named Kenny Lewis, a seventeen-year-old who would soon be heading to Moody Bible Institute for a preaching ministry. Despite having been a Christian since the age of seven, when I accepted Jesus as my Savior at Sunnyside Baptist Church during a revival, I was, like many teenagers and even some adults today, afraid to witness to others. The thought of approaching a complete stranger for this purpose was particularly daunting. Yet, that's precisely what Kenny asked me to do.

During the afternoons at Falls Creek, we had free time, and most students spent it swimming, hiking, playing sports, or simply hanging out and enjoying Icees. Early in the week, Kenny approached me, expressing that he saw leadership potential in me among the girls, and asked me to share my faith and witness to each girl in our cabin by the week's end. He also wanted me to engage in witnessing to students outside our cabin during the afternoons. I was gripped by fear at the prospect of speaking to these individuals, and "terrified" might better describe my emotions back then. I couldn't fathom why this fear held me. Despite having the Holy Spirit, I had never truly allowed Him to work through me. Additionally, coming from a different church, I didn't know the other kids in my cabin and felt like an outsider. How could Kenny perceive me as a leader?

Kenny encouraged me to pray about it and reminded me of the Bible verses, *"Not by might, nor by power, but by my spirit says the Lord of Hosts"* **(Zechariah 4:6b)** and *"I can do all things through Christ who strengthens me"* **(Philippians 4:13)**.

I was fully aware of my inability to do what he asked of me in my own strength. It was the first time I fully grasped what it meant to have the Holy Spirit living in me and working through me.

By Wednesday or Thursday, Kenny felt I was ready to go out witnessing on my own during the afternoons. By this time, I understood I had to rely entirely on the Holy Spirit speaking through me, as my strength would not suffice. As I ventured out, I prayed and trusted God to provide the words I needed. I approached a young man about my age who was standing near the refreshment stand, sipping on an Icee. I began witnessing to him about Jesus, and about 95% of the way through our conversation, I realized that I had no recollection of what I had just said. The Holy Spirit had proclaimed the gospel to this young man through me, and I had been entirely unaware of the words that had come out of my mouth. God had used me because I had surrendered my own efforts and made way for His power and Spirit to work through me.

I was both amazed and ecstatic as I comprehended that God had used me to convey His message despite how unprepared I had felt. That day marked the beginning of my intimate, close relationship with Christ. I learned that when

I relinquish my own abilities and admit my insufficiency, Christ promptly steps in, empowering me with His Spirit, who accomplishes the work through me as long as I get out of the way and let Him. I even had the opportunity to share my marvelous experience of being on fire for Christ and how He had worked through me that week in an article in the local newspaper, "The Broken Arrow Ledger," entitled "Girls Turned on at Baptist Camp." The feeling of having God speak through me that first time remains unforgettable, and I continue to cherish that profound intimacy with Him.

Years later, while Carl was pursuing his Master of Divinity degree at Southwestern Baptist Theological Seminary, he worked part-time on the church staff at Bethesda Baptist Church in Burleson, Texas, for a period. Like many Baptist congregations, this church had a weekly outreach program where we visited people in their homes to share the gospel with them. By this time in my life, I found this to be a rewarding experience, not only in participating but also in teaching others how to share their faith effectively. Consequently, I prayed for guidance from God to reveal the right person in the church to accompany me on an upcoming night of visitation. (Usually, I went with Carl, but he had other commitments that night.)

Through the prompting of the Holy Spirit, I noticed a young woman in the choir who was approximately my age at the time. This young woman was a familiar face in the church, a member known for her regular attendance. After the service, I approached her and asked if she would join me in visiting people in the neighborhood to explain how one can become a Christian. She expressed her willingness to help but mentioned her apprehension about discussing how to become a Christian with others. Having experienced a similar fear of sharing my faith as a teenager until I learned how the Holy Spirit could work through me, I understood her concern. I reassured her that she wouldn't need to do any speaking, as I would handle that part. Instead, I asked her to pray silently while we were in the home, knowing that this would be less intimidating for her.

On the agreed-upon day, we met at the church, and together, we went to the home of a middle-aged gentleman who had some loose connections to the church but did not attend regularly. After some initial conversation to establish rapport with him, I asked for permission to explain how he could be certain of going to heaven after his passing. He agreed, allowing me to provide a comprehensive explanation of our sinful nature, our inability to save ourselves, and how God had sent Christ as the perfect sacrifice for our sins through His death on the cross and resurrection from the grave. He even permitted me to use visual aids to ensure he grasped the message, including how to pray at that moment and invite Jesus Christ into his life as his personal Savior. I extended an invitation for him to accept Christ and become a Christian, but he declined, stating he wasn't ready. I thanked him for allowing me to share this important information and made sure he understood that he could reach out to us if he ever changed his mind or wanted to talk further.

I then turned to my friend to see if she was ready to leave. To my surprise, I found her with her head bowed in prayer. Although I had asked her to pray, I assumed she would do so with her eyes open. We headed to my car, and as we were about to back out of the driveway, she looked at me and said, "I was just saved in there. That was the clearest presentation of the gospel I've ever heard." I was so grateful for the Holy Spirit's work.

Being filled with the Holy Spirit refers to the experience of a believer being empowered, influenced, and led by the Holy Spirit. You receive the Holy Spirit when you become a Christian. He's like a birthday present when you are born into God's family. Being filled with the Holy Spirit is not a one-time event but an ongoing process. Believers are encouraged to continually seek the guidance, empowerment, and influence of the Holy Spirit in their lives. The Holy Spirit equips and empowers Christians to fulfill their roles and ministries within the body of Christ (the Church). This empowerment may manifest in various spiritual gifts and abilities, such as teaching, prophecy, healing, and others. Being filled with the Holy Spirit should result in the development of the "fruit of the Spirit." This includes love, joy, peace, patience, kindness, goodness, faithfulness, gentleness, and self-control (Galatians 5:22-23).

The Holy Spirit guides believers in making choices, discerning God's will, and understanding God's Word. Being filled with the Holy Spirit can provide believers with the courage to share their faith and stand up for their beliefs. The Holy Spirit can enhance a believer's experience of worship and prayer, helping them connect with God on a deeper level. The Holy Spirit assists in the process of sanctification, which is the ongoing transformation into Christlikeness. Believers become more and more conformed to the image of Jesus through the work of the Spirit. The Holy Spirit promotes unity among believers and within the Church. He helps foster a sense of community and cooperation.

Ultimately, being filled with the Holy Spirit is about having a deeper and more intimate relationship with God and living a life guided by His Spirit. During the process of recovering from grief, the Holy Spirit serves as a source of comfort and direction as you tread the challenging path of healing.

My challenge to you is to seek the filling of the Holy Spirit daily through surrender and submission to His leading. I urge you not to quench Him or ignore His influence. Thus, I implore you to actively seek this filling, aligning your actions with His divine direction.

Chapter 17:

Give Glory to God

When speaking to groups, I often pose the question, "What does God care about most?" In response, there are often various answers, including "the lost, " "His people," "shaping us to be more like Him, " and numerous other valid responses. While I concur that God cares about each of these aspects, I believe that what matters most to Him is His own glory.

What is God's glory? It's a concept that encapsulates the radiant beauty, majesty, and splendor of God. It encompasses His perfection, holiness, and magnificence. The glory of God is closely tied to His presence and the display of His attributes, which reveal His divine nature and character to humanity. It can be observed in the wonders of creation, the manifestations of His power and majesty, and the acknowledgment of His sovereignty and worthiness of worship. Ultimately, God's glory is an expression of His infinite greatness and the source of awe, reverence, and worship among believers. In essence, it's a testament to how spectacular He is. This is His intrinsic glory, and nothing we do can alter it, for it's an inherent part of who He is.

However, there is also a type of glory that is ascribed to Him. This is how we honor and worship Him. It involves giving Him credit for the changes He has made in your life, finding your satisfaction in Him, and offering Him praise. He deserves to be glorified by you, and it requires putting Him first because of His inherent worthiness.

Let's explore some Bible verses about God's glory to understand how this applies to you:

Psalm 19:1 (NIV) - *"The heavens declare the glory of God; the skies proclaim the work of his hands."* This verse illustrates how God's majestic creation magnifies His glory.

Psalm 24:7-10 (NIV) - *"Lift up your heads, you gates; be lifted up, you ancient doors, that the King of glory may come in."* It emphasizes that He is the King of Glory.

Isaiah 6:3 (NIV) - *"And they were calling to one another: 'Holy, holy, holy is the Lord Almighty; the whole earth is full of his glory.'"* This verse highlights how the earth reflects God's glory.

Exodus 33:18-19 (NIV) - *"Then Moses said, 'Now show me your glory.' And the Lord said, 'I will cause all my goodness to pass in front of you, and I will proclaim my name, the Lord, in your presence.'"* It shows that God's glory encompasses His goodness, and acknowledging His goodness is a way to give glory to Him.

Romans 11:36 (NIV) - *"For from him and through him and for him are all things. To him be the glory forever! Amen."* This verse affirms that He deserves glory because all things were created by Him and for Him.

1 Chronicles 16:24 (NIV) - *"Declare his glory among the nations, his marvelous deeds among all peoples."* You are tasked with declaring His glory to others and praising Him for His magnificent deeds.

1 Corinthians 10:31 (NIV) - *"So whether you eat or drink or whatever you do, do it all for the glory of God."* It emphasizes that your daily life, even simple activities like eating and drinking, should glorify God, which includes taking care of your body as His temple.

Psalm 104:31 (NIV) - *"May the glory of the Lord endure forever; may the Lord rejoice in his works."* Rejoicing in God and His deeds on your behalf brings Him glory.

Revelation 4:11 (NIV) - *"You are worthy, our Lord and God, to receive glory and honor and power, for you created all things, and by your will they were created and have their being."* This verse confirms that God deserves all glory, honor, and worship.

Isaiah 42:8 (NIV) - *"I am the Lord; that is my name! I will not yield my glory to another or my praise to idols."* It emphasizes that His glory is unmatched and should not be shared with any other. Seeking glory for yourself can lead to pride and separation from God. He alone deserves glory.

Psalm 96:8 (NIV) - *"Ascribe to the Lord the glory due his name; bring an offering and come into his courts."* You glorify God by offering Him praise, worship, gifts, and even your life.

Psalm 86:9 (NIV) - *"All the nations you have made will come and worship before you, Lord; they will bring glory to your name."* This verse acknowledges that God will ultimately receive glory from all nations, including you.

The prominent Christian theologian and pastor, John Piper, often states, "God is most glorified in us when we are most satisfied in Him." This phrase emphasizes that your pursuit of genuine and lasting satisfaction in God brings

Him the greatest glory. Your joy and contentment ultimately reflect the worth and desirability of God Himself. This concept emphasizes the importance of finding delight in God for His glorification.

You are here to manifest God's glory. He uses you and me to accomplish His work in this world. You must employ all possible means to share the message of Jesus Christ and His offer of salvation with others. You must yield to the Holy Spirit, allowing Him to narrate His story through your life. By sharing your own stories, you help others build their faith in God. You must firmly believe that a life bringing glory to God is what pleases Him the most. To lead a life that brings glory to God, daily surrender to Him is essential. This daily surrender leads to a transformative process in your life, revealing His glory.

I believe that Jesus Christ came into the world to be our Savior, and we see the full manifestation of God's glory in Him. He is the sole path to salvation. Each one of us is a sinner and in need of salvation. Jesus is the only way to attain it. To receive eternal life, you must believe in Him, placing your complete faith and trust in Him. You must acknowledge that He came to earth to save you from your sins and that He died on the cross for you. It also involves turning away from your past sins to embrace the new life He offers. This transformation leads to receiving the Holy Spirit and the opportunity for Him to work through you in this world. You realize that Jesus Christ offers a rich and purposeful life to anyone who completely trusts in Him and seeks Him for salvation and transformation. Knowing that He holds the answers to life's toughest questions, you can turn to Him in every situation.

So, what does all of this mean for you? How can you give glory to God? To glorify Him, you must acknowledge His goodness, share your testimony of who He is, and trust in Him for salvation and during times of trial. Avoid the trap of seeking glory for yourself, as it can lead to pride and separation from God. Instead, let your life bring glory to Him, remembering that He alone deserves all glory and praise. Are you seeking satisfaction in your accomplishments or worldly pursuits? True satisfaction comes from delighting in God and magnifying Him through your words and actions.

My challenge to you is to recognize that you were created to give God glory. Strive to find genuine satisfaction in Him. Avoid chasing after worldly things or false gods in search of satisfaction. Cease pursuing recognition or credit for yourself. Instead, give God credit for who He is and what He does. Honor Him by choosing to follow Him exclusively, letting your life reflect His greatness, and dedicating your heart entirely to Him.

Chapter 18:

Discipline Your Mind

What occupies your thoughts throughout the day? Are they filled with sadness and sorrow, or do they center on God's promises? How do you perceive yourself in the eyes of God? It's crucial to recognize that your thoughts shape your emotions, character, and actions. Controlling your thoughts is a skill you must cultivate. This can be particularly challenging after a loss, but with the guidance of the Holy Spirit, your mind can undergo a transformation, aligning with the mind of Christ.

Philippians 4:8 (NIV) advises, *"Finally, brothers and sisters, whatever is true, whatever is noble, whatever is right, whatever is pure, whatever is lovely, whatever is admirable – if anything is excellent or praiseworthy – think about such things."*

Proverbs 23:7a (NIV) emphasizes, *"As a person thinks in their heart, so they are..."*

Romans 12:2 (NIV) encourages believers, *"Do not conform to the pattern of this world, but be transformed by the renewing of your mind. Then you will be able to test and approve what God's will is — his good, pleasing and perfect will."*

In a sermon by John Stonestreet titled "How Not to Read Your Bible," he delves into **Isaiah 55:8-9 (NIV)**: *"For my thoughts are not your thoughts, neither are your ways my ways," declares the Lord. "As the heavens are higher than the earth, so are my ways higher than your ways and my thoughts than your thoughts."* Contrary to common interpretation during difficult times, Stonestreet suggests your thoughts and ways should align with God's.

How can you achieve this alignment? Refer back to the truths presented earlier in this book. Dwell on God's truth without distorting its meaning. Negative thinking, often referred to as "stinkin' thinkin'" by the late Zig Ziglar, is a failure to focus on the truth of God's Word, allowing the lies of the enemy to influence your thoughts.

In the context of grief, negative thoughts may include beliefs like "I will never get over this" or "It's my fault." It's essential to combat such patterns with the truth: God is sovereign over our lifespans, and blaming oneself or others is often rooted in unhealthy thinking.

First of all, we discussed in a previous chapter that God is sovereign over our lifespans. There is nothing you could have done that would have changed the outcome if it was time for your loved one's life to end. All the days of your life are also written in God's book, and you can't add to or take away from them. So it's not your fault. It was just their time. God has forgiven you if you belong to Him, and you need to learn to forgive yourself.

Forgiveness plays a crucial role in reshaping your thought patterns. Matthew 5:23-24 (NIV) emphasizes the importance of reconciling with others before offering gifts at the altar. Additionally, the Lord's Prayer in Luke 11:4 (NLT) emphasizes forgiveness of others as connected to your own forgiveness by God: "And forgive us our sins, as we forgive those who sin against us."

Whether grieving a loss or facing other challenges, transforming your thinking is essential. The Scriptures provide a foundation for this transformation. Depression, often stemming from unforgiveness, can be debilitating. Recognize the importance of aligning your thoughts with God's Word and seeking help if needed.

If you've never accepted Jesus as your Savior, consider a simple prayer to invite Him into your life. If you are already a believer but find yourself in a state of brokenness, reaffirm your commitment to Jesus, seeking His restoration. You must forgive others for any wrongs or perceived wrongs that they have done to you or your loved one. This might include family members, nurses, doctors, or even someone with a gun. Sometimes, if your loved one's death was due to suicide, you might have to forgive them. You might need to write it in a letter and make a sincere apology, and if necessary, mail it. You could burn it if they are not alive to receive the mail. Forgiveness is to clear your conscience and fix your attitude and thinking more so than for the other person. It is quite likely that they did something horrible to offend you, but you must learn to forgive it so you can move forward with your life. You don't want to be stuck in this bad place for years to come.

When you are involved in reading the scriptures on a regular basis, you begin to think like Jesus thinks. He is the most loving and forgiving person. He expects you to be like Him. That's the process of sanctification. It's becoming more like Him as you conform your life to what He tells you in scripture. Your thinking needs to change. If you are continually dwelling on things that were done to you, you are not able to clearly focus on the good God that we have and how He had a plan and a purpose even in the loss of someone's life. Your thinking needs to align itself with the Bible. This may be difficult, but you can write Scriptures on index cards, memorize them, and repeat them over and over until you actually believe them. Believing a lie or dwelling on some degrading thought is not where God wants you. He wants you to have a clear conscience before Him and before others. If you live out your life in quiet desperation, you will have a fruitless life, and you will be depressed and live in despair. This is never what God wants for his children.

Depression is one of the worst medical conditions. It leads to all kinds of sorrow and pain and can lead to many other medical problems and suicide. Most of the time, it stems from unforgiveness either towards someone else or towards God. You may feel that God was responsible for the way the situation is, and you can't even forgive Him. This is a sad and miserable state. You do not want to live in this state. Life is hard, but God is good. Unfortunately, if you do not focus on the faithfulness of God even in the midst of sadness, sorrow, or despair, then you have little hope of getting totally better.

Maybe you're grieving the loss of a marriage, the loss of fertility, or the loss of your health. I know I started grieving a couple of years before Carl went to heaven because I knew that the cancer was going to take his life. Fortunately, I was wise enough to speak to a Christian counselor who helped me to see that there was no loss yet. Your mind can conceive of things that you shouldn't even be thinking. It only leads down the wrong path towards more sadness and depression. You must change your thinking.

This is one of the most difficult chapters for me to write because even though I never went down this path, I have seen multiple patients, friends, and family members go down this path. It is a very devastating and destructive path. One of the things that many of them have in common is they don't know Jesus as their Savior. The truth is God has a perfect design for your life, and you have departed from it due to sin in your life. This leads to a state of brokenness. You may try to fix the brokenness by yourself by turning to alcohol, drugs, thoughts of suicide, more education to get a better job, a new relationship, or some other method. However, each of those things pulls you back into more brokenness.

You need a rescuer, someone who can rescue you from this situation. His name is Jesus. He came down from heaven and lived a perfect life and died on the cross for your sins. Then, He rose from the dead, proving that He was God and victorious over the grave and over sin. Turning to anything but Jesus leads towards more brokenness because any new relationship or addiction may look like it is temporarily helping, but it will snap you back like a bungee cord into more brokenness. If you trust in Jesus as your Savior, by turning from your sin and agreeing with God about it, and believing that Jesus did die on the cross for you and that He rose from the dead, you can be saved from this brokenness. You can do that in a simple prayer. You can say something like this:

"God, I know that I have departed from your perfect design for my life because of sin in my life, and now I am broken. I need you to rescue me. I believe that Jesus died on the cross for my sins and that He rose from the dead. Please forgive me. I am very sorry for my sin. Please come into my life right now and make me a new creature who is able to pursue Your perfect design for my life. Thank you for loving me and for dying for me. Thank You for giving me salvation right now. I want to follow You for the rest of my life. In Jesus' name I pray, Amen."

Friend, if you prayed that prayer and meant it in your heart, then Jesus came into your life right now in the form of the Holy Spirit. He gives you the ability to recover from your brokenness and to pursue His perfect design for your life. All of your problems will not go away immediately. Sin always has consequences, and some of those consequences will still be there. However, with the Holy Spirit living in you, you will be able to move forward through your grief, despair, and depression to follow his perfect plan for your life.

If you were already a follower of Jesus and had previously asked him into your heart and life, brokenness can still occur in your life. In this case, you need to do the same thing. You need to repent, turn from your sin, and trust Jesus completely to restore you. I've seen many Christians who need to do this because they have fallen into brokenness for whatever reason, and they need to turn back to Jesus and follow his perfect plan for their lives again.

Trusting in Jesus doesn't fix everything immediately, but through the process of sanctification, diligent prayer, Bible study, and involvement in a biblically sound church, you can control your mind towards correct thinking.

My challenge to you is to discipline your mind to correct thinking. You can do this first and foremost by becoming a follower of Jesus or renewing your commitment to follow Him. Then, you must reprogram your mind with the truth from His Word and daily prayer. You must memorize promises from His Word.

If you are one of the people struggling with wrong thinking, you may need to see a counselor or a doctor and get on some medication. My hope and prayer for you is that you will address this most essential issue now. Contact me through www.for-gods-glory.com for further information and support.

One Last Message!

My life is filled with joy and adventure again. God used the time of grieving and loss to show me His faithfulness and goodness to me. It's been four years since Carl went to heaven. I'm thriving and have such a deep love for God. He is so close to me, and I spend all day enjoying His presence, talking with Him, and worshiping Him.

Romans 8:28 (NIV) states: *"And we know that in all things God works for the good of those who love Him, who have been called according to His purpose."*

I wanted to live to a ripe old age with Carl by my side. That didn't happen. However, God has worked in and through me in so many different ways over these past four years. He used this time to draw me closer and start me on a different path to bring Him glory. By moving forward through my grief to a more intimate relationship with Him, I realized that He did work everything out for my good and

His glory. It was hard to see that at first. Now, I see it very clearly. He will do that for you too.

This book has been my journey from grief to bringing God glory. The process of regaining my focus on God, talking to Him, and listening to Him through His Word has been the key. I've attempted to bring you along on this journey. I hope you have joined me. The missing piece of the puzzle that you were searching for is Jesus. He was there all along, but you may not have noticed Him because you were focused on yourself and felt sorry for yourself. Maybe you were drowning in sadness and loneliness. Perhaps you were becoming a workaholic hoping to keep busy so you wouldn't have to think about your loss.

Thank you for joining me on this journey. It is my hope and prayer for you that you are leaving this time with me on a new trajectory for a hope-filled future. I would hate to think that you are still stuck. Dear friend, grief is a process that you go through. You are not to remain stuck in it. If you discover that you still need help, contact me at www.for-gods-glory.com. I will be happy to do private coaching with you.

My life's purpose is to know and enjoy God and help others know and love Him. If you are still struggling, please be willing to say so and get the help you need. Knowing Jesus is the greatest adventure there is. I don't want you to miss out on all the excitement and joy that is found in Him.

Acknowledgments

Through the years, many have shared ideas, mentoring, and support that have impacted my life, each in a different way. It's impossible to thank everyone, and I apologize to anyone not listed. Please know that I appreciate you greatly.

Most of all, I want to thank God for bringing me through grief to where I am now, glorifying You again. You are my life!

I would sincerely like to thank Amy Cruce for the time she spent reading and editing the content of this book. Your comments and suggestions helped to make the finished product better. I am thankful for the pictures you took for my book cover. You are deeply loved.

I would like to thank Bill Cordrey for all the wise counsel, prayers, and encouragement that helped me recover from grief and go forward in God's plan for my life. You were always available to talk and pray with me, and I deeply appreciate you for being such a good friend. I cannot say enough about how much you helped me. You and Piper Cordrey have been a continued source of encouragement.

I would like to thank my friends in Oklahoma, Earl and Nancy Stephenson, Gayle and Bob Jones, and Mary Jane and Mike Collins, who helped me with my grief in the early stages of recovery by hosting me in their homes, encouraging me, and helping me see my way forward by being such good friends in my time of need. I especially want to thank Nancy for mobilizing her widow friends at FBC Weatherford to show love and care for me as a new widow by giving me advice and Scriptures to cling to.

I am deeply grateful for the prayers of my church family at Rock Bridge Baptist Church in Norcross, Georgia, and for Dianne Sheintal, who prays with me weekly. You have encouraged me, and I know that you love me. I sincerely appreciate your prayers and encouragement.

My extended Hulsey family has been faithful in traveling and spending time visiting with me. I have relied on you for love, prayers, and encouragement. You are such a wonderful family, and our Zoom calls, trips together, numerous text messages, and prayers mean so much to me. I am especially grateful to my six siblings and their families because you know I could talk forever, especially when I was lonely, yet you still listened. I deeply love you all.

I am especially grateful for my Georgia family. Joyce Barrington, you have prayed for me and encouraged me. I am so appreciative. My precious daughter, Michelle Leggett, thank you for fixing photos, reading and editing part of the book, and all the time you spent doing that late at night. I love you more than you can even imagine. Thank you to Benjamin and Michelle Leggett for allowing me lots of time with Theo and Autumn. That time of making memories and traveling together is priceless. Theo and Autumn Leggett, I deeply love all the smiles, hugs, kisses, and pure joy that you give me. You are so precious to me, and I am grateful for your love.

About Pat

Pat Barrington is a widow who was married for 41 years prior to her husband's trip to heaven. She was born and raised in Oklahoma and went to the University of Oklahoma, which is where she met her late husband, Carl. She is a retired Family Practice Physician who loves to travel and has visited 103 countries. She goes on mission trips at least twice a year, and often, they are medical and evangelism trips where she is thrilled to work with her team, telling others about Jesus.

Pat enjoys speaking for groups and leads the Women's Ministry Team at Rock Bridge Baptist Church in Norcross, Georgia, where she is a member. She also teaches a ladies' Sunday school class, and she is a leader in the Drive-Through Prayer ministry. Pat has one daughter, Michelle, and two grandchildren, Theo and Autumn. She currently resides in Lawrenceville, Georgia.

*Special **FREE** Bonus Gift for You*

To help you to achieve more success, there are **FREE BONUS RESOURCES** for you at:

www.for-gods-glory.com

- 3 in-depth videos that will lead you to a life in Christ that honors and glorifies Him

Made in the USA
Columbia, SC
13 October 2024